Dear Kitchen Saints

[Cover Photo – Connie with her husband Jim.]

Dear Kitchen Saints

Letters from an Iowa Housewife

By Connie Hultquist

The Legacy of Home Press
puritanlight@gmail.com

The Legacy of Home Press
ISBN-13: 978-0615834153
ISBN-10: 0615834159
Dear Kitchen Saints – Letters from an Iowa Housewife

Author – Mrs. Connie Hultquist
Compiled and Edited by – Mrs. Sharon White

Subject: Marriage; Homemaking; Frugal Living; Poverty; Christian Living; Housewife; American Family History.

Contents

The Letters {Part II}   - Entering Widowhood-

The Letters {Part III}   - April 2013 Reflections-

Appendix

Preface

In 2000, Connie's marriage testimony went all over the world, through Nancy Campbell, in *Above Rubies* Magazine. It was published under "anonymous," but included an email address. Many wives in hurting homes contacted Connie to thank her for sharing the article. Many also asked for help and support because of their own troubles.

Connie, a housewife of humble means, had been married for twelve years to a man who left her repeatedly and spent time in prison. Despite the pain and hurt and trials she went through, the reward came when her husband was saved. Together, they were married for almost 40 years, raised 6 children, and have an incredible lifelong testimony. With her husband's blessing, Connie sent in her anonymous testimony, which gave hope to wives everywhere.

A small group had been set up to receive Connie's daily writings. After the testimony was published, she became a much needed Titus 2 mentor. Her "hillbilly" wisdom helped counter the Prosperity Gospel and Christian Feminist movement.   She was able to encourage hurting wives and mothers to focus on their husbands and children, with a great faith in God.

Helpers came along and set up a yahoo group, to organize the writings that were being sent out to hundreds of women. Soon there was a website, and then a Facebook page.

In 2013, Connie's testimony was republished in *Above Rubies*, with an update. This time, she included her name. A new generation of young wives and mothers needed her encouragement.

This book is a sampler collection of Connie's writings. It is our hope that readers will glean much wisdom from these letters. These are from as early as 2002 to 2013. The process of editing this book must be explained:

- Editing the work to meet proper English standards was never the goal. Connie's style of communicating has a certain voice that needs to remain strong. Her writings have become a treasured piece of History.

- Seeking out a selection of writings took many hours and much labor.

- Next, formatting it from emails into a book, took a tremendous amount of effort. For most of the years, Connie had been writing on a little email machine. This machine only allowed a certain number of words in each letter. To save space, Connie used words such as "wud" instead of "would." She also wrote many letters in "Parts." Instead of wasting the limited room she had on paragraphs, she creatively used a series of periods (. . .) to separate thoughts, and to help the reader to pause. Much of this will remain in the text.

In the following pages you will step into the home of an Iowa housewife. You will feel as if she is writing directly to you about her daily life, and about the common traps in our culture that want to lure wives and mothers away from true Christian homes. Many, who have known her through the years, by her letters, call her "*Mother Connie*." Her godly wisdom, and sweet sense of humor, will echo in your memory for years to come.

- The Publisher, May 2013

The Letters

{Part I}

- Marriage, Home, and Family-

1

Barefoot in the Garden

Dear Sisters of the Land, Yesterday I didn't get any quiet time to write in my garden journal or write down my garden dreams. Today I plan to cook this morning and get something in the oven and out of the way so that I can make a mess with my papers and gardening books this afternoon... In the spring, after the garden is tilled, I love to plant my beans in the rain. ... barefooted OF COURSE.

I make a long furrow with my hoe ...uncover the earth, and drop my bean seeds in one by one. Then with my right foot I toss the dirt over the top.. then step down on it and next, my left foot and step on that...walking backwards down the row. As I put my seeds in the furrow the rain sprinkles each seed. I love to plant a garden in the rain.. the earth is so yielding and forgiving. It's like us when we weep and are so vulnerable ..we invite precious seeds from the Lord into our hearts. Tender hearts .. forgiving hearts, are so precious to Jesus.

About the time I am so muddy I can hardly walk another row..Papa will yell for me out the back door. "Telephone," Or, "We have company." Then reality hits and I say to myself, "Connie your fingernails are black. Why didn't you stick your nails in a bar of soap before you went outside? It will be a week before your hands look right again." I don't worry that people will see me soaking wet in my garden.. but my fingernails are sort of embarrassing in the spring and summer. Oh I love the rain on my long hair...it makes it so soft and gentle . As the rain falls on my hair, I think of how the Lord is washing the worldliness from my glory ..A soft warm spring rain is so comforting and healing to both the gardener and the earth and its seeds. I need the winter to hibernate and rest but when the spring comes it is, to me, like a new morning. Everything is fresh.. and so much work to do to prepare for the planting season.

Papa is so weary of the winter.. he seemed so tired as he left for work this morning. The spring is like a tonic to him ... he will feel the joy when it finally comes. This winter has been especially hard and long and it seems the darkest now.. just before the dawn of a new morning. It's definitely a day to dream and plan in front of my south living room window. The rays of the sun in the afternoon streaming through my angel wing begonia in the window is so comforting.. a wonderful place to dream of spring. Weeping lasts for the night .. but joy comes in the morning.

2

Christian Feminists

Dear Mothers, My fingers just tremble when I type on my key board about Christian Feminists.. It's such a lie and so destructive.. I was watching the 700 club this afternoon.. I like to watch the news......Well after the news, they started telling about a women's Christian movement that was supposed to be like Promise Keepers for Men.. So, one dear little woman gets on there and she says that she was glad she found this group ...All she used to do was think of her family and never of God.. All she thought of was fixing meals for her husband and the children, etc....So she had to leave her family behind and go get with this women's group.. ...As if Jesus couldn't be found at home? Or that she couldn't have made that decision without 5,000 women? Or after she got with the 5,000 women and the light bulb went on that she had to put God first (??), couldn't she have left and gone home? And the women that organized the thing sure weren't home caring for their families...and probably hadn't been in months...And they are there to talk about priorities (?), and putting God first? All of this is like someone going up to Jesus, in Bible days, and saying, "Jesus you work so hard with these people, preaching and teaching and healing the sick, come away from your burdens and get with the religious group of the day and hoop and holler and just plain have fun..Put yourself first for once. Let your hair down..All work and no play makes God a dull God.. Dull? Yes ...sometimes.. burdensome? Yes ..Suffering? Yes.. Self sacrificing? Yes you bet.. But what did Jesus say to those who tried to call Him away from His work? He said, "I must be about my Father's business."

The speakers for this group of women walked on stage.. Oh yes the classic older women ..Modern and business - like. Not about to stay home and care for family or babysit for grand-babies..They aren't doing it and they are teaching yet another group of mothers how to not do it....And all in Jesus' name.. God forgive us.

Deception rules these women with an iron rod.. And I can just see these speakers as they travel the universe with the message of how to put yourself first.. while lying and saying you are putting God first.. I can see me joining the group.. being a speaker.. "Sorry Papa, I won't be home for about 2 weeks..I am a key speaker on how to put God first." The first few weeks Papa may buy that.. the 2nd two weeks probably not. The 3rd two weeks I would get home and everyone would be gone...including Papa... I mean the man loves me ..but he would only put up with that stuff for awhile..Papa is not a preacher..He loves the Lord and I would rather have him as a prayer partner than anyone I know.. He is a powerful man of prayer.. A little rough around the edges.. But he has mountain moving faith... And in most ways he has more common sense than I have.. But he puts family first...and he expects me to do the same.

Putting family first is obvious in the Bible .. A man called into the ministry is one who has his family in order first.. The men called to leave the family for Christ's sake? He is not a man who is deserting his family.. he is leaving a humble loving family and it is a sacrifice to him.. Not a time for him to enjoy putting his interests above his families.. A wife is to submit to her husband as unto the Lord.. ..

3

Old Home Remedies

Dear ladies, Got my Jim off to work, and I'm back to share some family Home remedies. When raising my babies, I was always just an old fashioned mother. What was good for my great grand mother was good enough for me. I always made sure my children were dressed warm when they went out in the cold. And at night in the winter time, I would wake up and check them to make sure they were warm. Hats, Ladies... the children need their hats. Earaches are caused from children being out in the cold without their hats. I never had to take any of my 6 children to the doctor for earaches. Even in the spring or the summer, for that matter, when the children were babies, we mothers put hats on their heads. They were nylon and light weight for the warm weather. I mean if there was a wind blowing, we never allowed the wind to enter our baby's ears. If the children did get an earache in the winter, I would use sweet oil dropped into their ears.

Dan would come in bawling after playing outside in the snow. "Mom, my ear hurts." I would help him get his wet clothes off and put his mittens and hat on the hot air register. I would stop what I was doing and put my attention on Danny. "Come on Danny I will sit with you and put the oil in your ear." I would sit on the couch with a bed pillow on my lap... he would lay down with the hurting ear up and the well ear resting on the pillow. Then I would pour a little sweet oil into his ear, and then I would have a warm wash cloth ready for him to hold over his ear. I had him lay there for maybe a half an hour.. so that the oil would go down deep in his ear. It always worked for us... of course I always prayed for him too. But we never had health insurance so we had to do the home remedies. We still don't have insurance and we are hardly ever sick.

I believe that prevention is the key to keeping children well. I never really allowed sick children around my children either. And if one of my children was sick, I made sure no one else drank out of the same cup the sick child had. I am really particular about that still.

I made my own cough syrup and it really works. It's all natural so you can take it every half hour if you need to until the child's coughing stops. Just take a jar and fill it half full with the Real Lemon in the green bottle at the store? Then fill your jar the rest of the way with honey. Shake it up really well, and that is it. I would give my children a few tablespoons of it at a time. And if my children were sick .. we didn't go anywhere. If my children got really sick I always went in another room and cried, they were so close to me. As adults now, my older children who live out of town, still call me if they are real sick. But if the children were sick it was a really sober time for me, especially. I would just lay my life down and care for my children. Of course Papa had to go to work so he couldn't nurse them, but I could and I did. If it had of been life and death, we would have taken them to the doctor.... but it never came to that. Our first three, I took to the doctor because we could. We had insurance. But the 2nd three, I didn't. My last 3 children never have been to the doctor for common colds or viruses. Mary had to go earlier this year for an asthma attack ... I could have doctored her at home but she was scared and so we had to go. Another Home remedy and then I should close and get Mary up for school. For asthma attacks this is what I used to do with Mary. She would, as a child, start to get hyper and then get short of breath. I would make her calm down and would give her a pain reliever and that would stop it. . . .

4

Women's Conferences

Dear Mothers , Someone asked me to write about what I
think about all the fellowship Christian women seem to need...
So here is my 2 cents worth..Ya know, the King's mother
speaks wisdom to him in Proverbs 31..She says, "Don't give
your strength to women..or your ways to which destroy kings."
And we women who are serious about building a home for the
Lord shouldn't be caught dead at those retreats..Why would ya
want to go there and leave the baby behind and your husband
and become one with a bunch of silly women? The Titus 2
Mother's ministry is to help you back to your husband and
children. The older Mother is to teach you to love your home
and children and to be a keeper at home..She is to be like a
midwife that helps you to birth your baby. A midwife doesn't
come in to take over the husband's role as Priest and

teacher..She comes in as a helper to the family..The Titus 2 ministry is to be like this..the older Mother is to help lead the wife back under her husband's authority.

I write daily because of the lies in the world and the cult religions out there..The Pioneer women didn't need a daily teaching..They had grown up with it and knew their roles. But now we live in Sodom and Gomorrah and daily the voice of the world tells women that the home isn't where they are taught to know the Lord..We think we aren't taught at home or taught by our husbands because we get so down and depressed..{"he isn't meeting my needs?" kind of thing}And we think if we are down and depressed that we need to take a hike to a WOMEN'S RETREAT. Those speakers get ya all full of joy bubbles and singin' and dancin' and clappin' and hootin' ..Then it's time to come home and back to reality.. You walk in the bathroom and husbands undershorts are STILL on the floor and life ain't so fancy at home..Nobody is singin' and dancin' and hootin'..Well ya know, I think of the woman I read about once who lived out on the Prairie. Her husband was gone for about 2 weeks to get supplies and her occupation all day was to take clubs and beat wolves away from her door ..The wolves were hungry and it was winter.. If Mother hadn't beat them to death they would have eaten her children..I mean this went on for days, the wolves just kept coming..But she did keep her family safe while her husband was away..Now let me see..That woman could have used a Retreat if anyone could..But she didn't leave her family and she wasn't happy and singin' while she was beating wolves to death all day..This woman did what she had to do ..I know she didn't like it..But we mothers think that if all isn't sunshine and roses that we should run out the door to church ..Well ya know what? If I did all of that I wouldn't have a marriage right now..Our husbands pretty much see through that deception even if we don't.

Always throughout history the Mother has set the spiritual temp. of the home. .Mother is to pray and she is the foundation of the home's peace..She is to keep the home..this is her place of authority..She needs to rise while it is yet night and prepare for her family in the physical and the spiritual realm..When her husband gets up and greets her she should have some basic word from the Lord first..Mother should live a holy life in the home..She should be prudent and full of courage and righteousness. She should learn a pattern of good works and be dutiful..You won't learn this at a retreat..You learn obedience through your suffering.

What would that Pioneer Mother who had just beat 100 wolves to death say about a retreat? Well she would probably think, "Wow what a deal let me at it!" ..But then she would say, "Well who will take care of the children and my husband?" Common sense would kick in and she would think differently. We must arm ourselves with duty.

5

Women's Retreats

Often these retreats teach a woman to be dissatisfied in her home..They try to teach her to use her gifts outside her home..The truth of this is that unless a Mother and Wife learns the truth of her husband's spiritual authority, then the Lord won't give her His gifts anyway..She will get gifted all right at the women's meetings. But they will be gifts of witchcraft. She goes back home with her gifts and she learns how to throw her husband off his authority. I have known many powerful women in my life and always they are women who respect the man's place in the home..Dixie was very submissive and Jill R. was too..And Mary L. in her 70's is very submissive to her husband..And I am telling you, if I need prayer and go to Mary L. and ask her to pray, then it's as good as done..Mary L. is a woman of prayer and knows authority in the spiritual realm. But most women will not take up this cross and follow Christ.

If they can't have the joy bubbles? Then forget the rest..You won't find a flock of virtuous women anywhere....God spreads them out..I have only known a few women who are really called to be the virtuous woman..Many start out good but fall along the way as they get older..It's rare to find an older Titus Mother..Many call themselves one but to find a real one is hard to find..Most women want the touchy - feely bubbles in their religion that hits the flesh and not the spirit. They don't want to take on the armour of God and live a holy life of separation unto God..They want to be seen and petted and praised.

A woman that will not fall for these lies is a rare woman indeed. A Mother who can get up in the morning and take on the home with a sense of duty is a powerful woman..Most women want to get up and run out the door and forsake her home duties..And she thinks if her husband doesn't go along with her, then he is a dirty son of a gun..Christian stay-at-home Mothers are the worst!! They refuse to be strapped at home and to home duties.. This is so sad as the Christian husband continually comes home after work to an empty home and a cold kitchen...NO supper even started ..He is hungry and needs the comfort of a sweet wife, a clinging vine who has been waiting for him to comfort her..And if husband says one word about, "where were you ..I couldn't find you?" Then he is classified as a big baby who couldn't make his own supper..That is sad and some of you Christian women are so guilty of doing this..And you should be ashamed of yourselves..You should pray and weep with intercessions to the Lord..Ask Him to forgive you for wanting only your flesh to be satisfied. Ask the Lord to help you to be a submissive wife and Godly Mother..We women need to grow up and take on our home duties as strong trusted Mothers and Wives.

Don't look at what the world thinks about you or what the church ladies think..Look at your husband and see your life through his eyes..I have always said about myself.."If I can't please one man in my life and can only please women then what good am I?" We are women who are called as Helpers to men ..not helpers to women..To hell with what the neighbour woman or your mother- in- law thinks of ya. Please your husband even if he is a drunk and druggy..Get down in his ash heap with him. Understand him..Be a helper to him and help him up..I mean if you are such Hot Stuff then why can't ya help your husband? If you can't help the man God has set before you to help, then who else can you help? God has set you in a place to be taught in the home..If your gifts of the Spirit aren't working in the home, then they won't work anywhere else either..If you can't learn the basic teachings of patience and duty, then God can't use you anywhere else in ministry..Your unruly husband will either make or break you as a woman of God..

6

Puttering

Dear Mothers, I am up in the night writing..I will have Baby Rose today, the joy of my life. The last time we had her, I dressed her in a handmade prairie dress I had gotten at a sale..It was from the 1970's ..a yellow calico..Also a prairie sun bonnet..She looked like a Little House on the Prairie child..And she still has potatoes and balls mixed up..So she takes a potato outside to throw about like a ball. It sounds so funny as we are playing and I say to her, "Go get your potato." It's nice as potatoes don't roll down the street and Gram doesn't have to chase them ..Baby will say "Ball" and throw the potato up in the air.

And ya know I was just praying in the chair this morning..And I just told the Lord how thankful I am for my cooking and baking things. I am so grateful that I have a private kitchen to cook in ..and ya know, if we have husbands who will work for us and let us stay home, then we really have a lot to thank the Lord for..I love all of my cooking utensils ..My favorite things I guess are my enamel spoons for stirring. I have a nice collection of them. .And I love looking for them when I go to Garage sales..I have about a dozen spoons all sizes..Mostly, they are the red with specks of white dots..and the dark blue..But I have gotten some lately that are the sort of light blue..I would love to find some of the light green ones that date back to the early 1900's. For mixing up muffins or biscuits I like a small spoon; not the biggest mixing spoon.. I like the spoon to be smaller if I am using a smaller crock bowl to stir in. My big grayish blue mixing bowls are more favorites of mine..I just like to mix things by hand I guess and not get out my electric mixer...Of course I enjoy all the dishes the Lord has gotten for me over the years. My Grandmother loved dishes..Mom used to say that when Gram fixed a meal she managed to use every dish in the house..And when Gram and Mom would go to town to shop, Gram always bought a dish at the Dime Store before she came home..The Old time Dime stores were the fun stores when I was a kid..And they always had pretty serving bowls to use for the table..It was just a bowl to serve a can of peas or green beans in to set on the table..Mother never baked bread. But she always got out a bread plate to put on the table for my dad's white sliced store - bought bread.. Many of the women in the old days loved their dishes..And they were very careful to take good care of them to make sure they didn't get broken.

There used to be this word "Puttering?" ..When you would ask my Dad what he was doing in the garage with his tools, he would often say, "Oh, I am just puttering, just foolin' around." He loved working with his tools and arranging them and organizing them. Often he would start out puttering and then would fix something as his mind relaxed.. And often, the old time Mothers would do this in their kitchens..Sort of not really doing anything specific but many things in general..And as she puttered in her kitchen, the ideas would begin to flow..The old time Mothers thought that an organized kitchen meant an organized mind.

In my kitchen cabinets, I like the old fashioned look. I have taken brown paper sacks and made shelf paper..I crease it at the edge so the paper hangs over the shelf..then I would cut designs in it with my scissors. The old time Mothers used to do that with brown sacks or newspaper..I love the brown paper and use it..I found a neat glass bottle at a Sale ..I used it for buttons ..but it had no lid. So I took brown sack paper and made a covering for my button bottle and then tied brown string around it..Dan saw it and said, "Oh Mom, I love that." Another item I enjoy collecting is the old Country Living Magazines..I remember back in the 70's when those magazines first came out they were so anointed of God..If you can find some really old ones at sales you would love reading them. . .

7

Victory Wives and Mothers

Dear Sisters of Victory, Well I am boiling macaroni.. It's whole wheat... and takes a long time to get done. It's for goolash.. Boy am I tired.. I was up a few hours in the night last night with Mary. She had really bad cramps... Then I was up before 6 with Jim making his coffee, etc. Hopefully, I will get a nap this afternoon before Jim gets home from work. You know ladies, in the early years of my marriage... when life was so troubled? I never even dreamed that someday I would be a writer. Back in those old days, all I desired was to just have a husband that loved me and a father for my children. I never thought that someday I would write to many women who were going through the same things. All I did when I was alone was make a home for my children and prepare for Jim to be saved. People screamed at me to do something with my life... to get on with my life. But all I wanted to do was stay home and be a homemaker.

Older women told me I wouldn't amount to a hill of beans... Just staying home and looking after my children.... keeping house.. and just keeping food on the table. I was on state aid.... and I was embarrassed about that. We lived with a lot of lack. But I did not speak lack to my children. I just told them that I was hoping in God and they should too. I lived a simple private life with my children. I did some writing then but not very much. All Mary, Jesus' mother, ever did was live a simple life and raise the Lord Jesus Christ. Can't you imagine someone in this age worrying that she hadn't made anything of her life? All the mothers in the Bible basically lived as Mary did.... your children, dear Mothers, are as little Jesus' too. Be content to be just mothers to your children and hope in God for your husbands to come home.. to be saved. But be at Peace...trust in the Lord...What you are doing matters. Just like what I did mattered. To the world, I was doing nothing... to the Lord, I was being obedient. And He rewarded me. He gave me the desires of my heart.

Can you imagine how I have felt this 21 years later having my testimony go all over the world? And if you follow my example... you will be following a woman who supposedly didn't amount to anything. It matters to me that I amounted to something to suffering saints. I never wanted to be worldly anyway. I have never written a book and never want to either. I would be concerned that it would take away from my time as a wife and mother. My greatest desire in my heart has never changed through the years...still all I want is for my family to walk and talk with God. I stay here as an example to my older children . I want my boys to marry stay- at- home mothers. Mothers who will be a light in the darkness to my grandchildren. I don't want to stop with just seeing my husband saved and living an honest wholesome life.. I want to see my children marry Godly spouses and have solid homes where Christ dwells. Mothers, we only have one life to live for Christ... only what is done for Him will last. In my eyes, I will have failed as a mother if I don't pray all of my children into His Kingdom. .. I can't imagine living on this earth and not leading my children to Christ. I couldn't face Jesus on judgment day if I felt that the children I was responsible for didn't honor the Lord.... Susanna Wesley, a stay at home mother, was responsible for bringing revival to England.

8

Visiting by the Fireside with a Cup of Tea

Dear Mothers, Come sit with me by the fire this morning.. Let's have some coffee, or I have tea. ."herbal"..if that is what you would like...It's cold this morning..the fire will keep us warm.. let's just visit for a while before the children wake up and we must all get back to our home duties... My friend Lynetta came over last night to visit.. I was so glad to see her ...I wanted to pick at her brain a little and ask her what she thought of the current news..the terrorist attack..[9/11]...She told me that at first she watched a lot of TV news and then she knew the Lord was just saying to trust in Him..and she quit watching it... That is a good point...But our family, I guess, is so expressive...We are working through all of this by discussing it.. Jimmy, age 35, just moved away from New York this summer and our daughter, Christine, was just a 20 minute walk from the explosion. Of course, as you know, we have talked a lot about all of this back and forth long-distance on the phone.. Our family doesn't have cable so we don't get the news channels...I have received the News on the 700 club lately...I like a lot of what Pat Robertson says...I think his heart is turning to a true shepherd's heart.. He is looking after the sheep instead of looking after his money..I think this fear war has brought a lot of these prophets back to the Lord..Any time a man begs for money from the already hurting sheep, you know he is a false prophet..The shepherds are to look after the sheep as loving fathers.. as God's hand extended. Well I am finally seeing some of this.. Praise the Lord..

I have even heard that some of the Christian shows are telling the truth concerning the family..Praise the Lord..But one point I made to Lynetta last night and wanted to discuss with you is the following: While I like a lot of what is being said from the Christians, I think they are, at times, talking over my head economically.. I think there are some common sense things that every family can do ..should do...like storing water..I think a lot of men who are in authority are skipping over talking about these obvious preparations for the common family..because they are afraid of being laughed at.. The Y2K scare looked like at the time? When the lights DID go ON.. Jan 1, 2000? That anyone who saved water was a barefoot Hill

Billy...

Well I was saying last night, I think the Y2k preparation was very significant.. a part of the plan.. A lot of folks were right about the collapse of our society but their timing was off.. They knew something was going to "Go Boom" but they didn't know what.. Now it does seem our society is collapsing but later than the predictions...First of all, I am no one..no big authority..But just among us ladies I think we need to prepare just as we did for Y2k... I am a barefoot Hill Billy...I admit it...But sometimes God chooses the foolish to confound the wise.. Now Lynetta has a point that all this stuff could scare the life out of you and some folks SHOULD just forget the whole thing and trust in God... Because God has a calling for each of us..a place of duty ..different for each mother and family..I guess this morning I just wanted to encourage the mothers who feel the need to prepare to be strong and do what God has called you to do.. Also to not be intimidated by the fact that you had to throw out all of that water in the year 2000...

9

Depression Era Mothers

And ya know, some of the farm mothers during the
Depression era were able to feed their families well..They had
nothing but food..They had their own chickens and saved their
vegetable seeds from year to year and planted huge gardens. .
They started pots and containers of every kind with seedlings
in the winter for spring gardens.. (The city mothers didn't fare
nearly as well) ...The husband and his sons would hunt and
fish and bring home the meat for supper..Mama would sell
eggs to pay for material and sewing items..The cream from
milking "Bossy" wasn't used for the family meals as it was sold
in town ..or exchanged at the Grocery Store for coffee and
some tobacco for Papa...or just cash to buy postage stamps or

a gallon of gas for the car. And ya know one thing, those women didn't go out to work? And Mama made sure above all that she had coffee for her husband and tobacco for his pipe or for hand rolled cigarettes..I mean Mama kept her husband happy..And the women that didn't keep their husbands happy back then, paid in the long run..

I have read so many stories about men who couldn't feed their families and they would kill themselves..A man that couldn't feed his family was not even a man back then..And he figured he may as well kill himself and be one less mouth to feed..Or many men went out on the road to find work and never returned..The mother's job at home was precious and she was needed to sing to the family and to dry their tears..She was the star of the home and the strong shoulder to cry on..She was a woman of faith and courage ..And if she wasn't, she just flat lost her family..

And ya know, during the Dirty Thirties in Kansas they had no rain for 3 years..And so they had no gardens and mother kept her family alive on dried beans ..Mainly she kept them alive with her faith ..Also there were several plagues of grasshoppers during that time too ..The grasshoppers came and ate everything off the top of the ground. They would eat the wooden handles off the garden tools..Also, the land in Kansas was so over worked by the settlers..They had so few trees and when the wind came, it would blow the dry top- soil right off..So the Dust Storms were terrible..in that 3 years of no rain..So the Mothers homes were just full of dry dirt..They would have to shovel the dirt out of their homes in the country. In order to start supper, they had to first clean the dishes full of dirt..Mother was the anchor of the home as she kept the faith and encouraged the family to keep on goin'..

And now dear mothers, in our age you all have a job to do to keep your families happy and well fed and full of courage..WE need to keep the hope up in our families..We need to have homes that are festive and alive with joy..We too fight a war as the times about us are hard. Ya know, we need to take lessons from the Mothers of old..We need to cook and bake every day too..Mothers used to make pies and cakes once a week..Also a few batches of bread, depending on family size..We seem to be losing our families; and factories are feeding our loved ones..We need to fill up our cookie jars with homemade cookies and bring the joy and gladness back into our homes..I have had so many interruptions on this writing today.. I have been workin' on it since early this morning..I am just going to have to quit it and write again about it later.

10

Mother's Home Journal

Dear ladies, I hope you are enjoying your new Year. Today..
this morning, Jim and I will be going on a little trip out of
town to visit his sister ... a few hours from here. We are
looking forward to some time alone together. Mary wants to
stay home and do some things by herself too. So many things
are on my heart this morning.. Last night I was reading a book
on St Francis of Assisi and some other stories of martyrs. One
sentence read like this: Would you rather be able to speak to
the King or to His servants? Would you rather hear from the
King ... or from His servants? Often ... I want to hear from His
servants and the arm of the flesh rather than the King's voice. .

Sometimes I take it for granted that the Lord speaks to me... But in this world we cannot have it both ways. If we shut ourselves out from the world in order to keep our own temptations at a minimum...so we can hear Him more clearly....then we pay a price in loneliness. We cannot be a friend to this world and be a close friend to Christ. We don't shut ourselves away from the world because we ARE Holy... but because we are not holy. Because if we dance in the streets with the local pied piper who is leading the church ladies to Jezebel....then who will they turn to when they find out that Jezebel wasn't the answer?

Sometimes I want to take a flying leap into the streets and be a sister again as I once was to these ladies who follow every wind of doctrine. Just to feel a part of things I guess. In fact, I think lately I have been guilty of some of this.. And when I came back to myself and felt lonely for the King's anointing and presence ... I found that the King was strangely cool to me. Seeing the local church ladies playing both sides of the fence made everything look so easy .. I thought I could pull off the same thing. Well I could pull it off... yet lose the anointing. I found once I got back that it took me 4 hours to hear His voice whereas before I had easy access to His anointing.

This book I was reading also spoke of embracing poverty. Well how would that fit into today's doctrines of you must be rich to enter the kingdom of God? That, "poverty is a curse and riches a blessing." To me if we are not radicals for Christ in this present, sinful world ..then Darlin' we are backing up. Can

He use His daughters who only fellowship with each other and not first with the Father? Who are we and what is our place as mothers in this present world? He calls we daughters of God to a higher calling. He calls us to hear His voice and to live a life that is conducive to hearing and doing spiritual activities. We must be dutiful as Keepers at Home.....but first we must hear our instructions from the King of Kings.

The devil isn't playing ladies .....he will rip your guts out if he gets the chance. Can we mothers fight him with one foot in the world and one in the church? Depends on the church I guess. But as for me I want both feet planted on the Lord's mat that lays directly in front of His throne. I can't expose the worldly church of today when I write to magazines. I am just so happy though to tell the truth about it on my little email machine. Knowing Christ and His anointing......there is a price to pay.. If we want to be friend to God we will be enemies of this present world. The Lord is Spirit and truth and to walk with Him we must walk in the truth and in the Holy Spirit. Lately, I have missed the mark I feel. The Lord called upon me for service and I felt my lamp of oil was empty. . .

11

The Lady of the House

Dear Mothers, I want to write today about the strength of the virtuous woman of Proverbs 31..Most of the women in the Bible were published in the word of God for what they did concerning their homes..Their place of service is in the home..A woman of strength and dignity is ABLE to stay home..Some women could stay home to be a stay- at- home mother and wife..but they don't have the strength to stay home..The streets call them ..they want to leave the home and go play at the mall or someplace..any place but home..But the wise woman is powerful..She knows how to beat the devil at his own game ..She is wise and stops the foolishness of folks using her home like "The Do Drop In." She opens her mouth with wisdom and on her tongue is the law of kindness..She looks well to the ways of her house and eats not the bread of idleness. But ya know, when your best girlfriend comes to the door and you just promised the children that you would read to them at nap time? Do you have the Moxie to be honest and to tell your friend that you have to lay down with the children and read? And that you will call her after naps? Now I mean I think you will agree with me that is hard to do..I mean I don't do a very good job of this myself..But ya know, the virtuous woman can pull this off without a hitch because she is wise..

I think of Nehemiah. .I have been reading this book a lot lately.. He was trying to help God's people build up their homes again.. He gave them courage. Now they could have built the wall back up without Nehemiah. They had tools but not the courage...They needed a cheer leader ..someone to lead them on..And ya know, now it seems as never before, the Christian home is torn down ..And so many of you have everything you need to build your home and to make a nest for your family. But you lack the strength of the virtuous woman..I lack the strength too sometimes..But I am gaining on it as I write each day..And some of us older Mothers have been called as Nehemiahs to help God's women to build up their homes..We are called to impart to the young ones an energy and strength of faith..As Nehemiah, we are called to rally the young wives and mothers to tell them to fight for their families like N. did..He told them to hold a sword in one hand and a hammer in the other hand..The enemies of the faith came and tried to discourage the believers but they had discernment and they didn't believe the lies of the devil..They repented of their own sins and prayed diligently and kept on building the wall..And whether you are called to write as the Titus 2 Mother or called to just read the writings, it is all the same Lord God that leads us..

I am helped and encouraged as I write..And some of you on these groups have a calling as the Titus 2 Mother..And as you take this responsibility you will be fed spiritually as you obey God ..As you give, you will receive..I'm not perfect but God just uses me because He needs a good laugh..I am called to the palace of the King as the court jester ..Our family is a work in progress..I know He will make it alright because I obey Him and He won't go back on His word..The Titus Mother is to have her own family in order so, since the Lord doesn't want me to be a black eye on the body of Christ, He will make my family sane in the end..So in other words, it will all come out in the wash? I am sure He has called some true Titus mothers, who do have their family in order, but they wouldn't do what they were called to do, so He ended up having to use the court jester for the Titus 2 Mother....

12

Home Made Peace

Dear Mothers, just create peace in your home.....Then start your homemaking..I used to cook and bake in the mornings..This way I had the supper family meal on its way ..And if any big interruption in my day came, then I didn't feel so worried about supper..I always homeschooled in the mornings..But we did some chores before school as to keep the home restful for Papa..Our home had to be picked up and top cleaned before we started school. Sometimes our family meal was at noon..So I would get that about half done before I started school at 7:30 am..Husband has to be first no matter what else happens at home..If you put the husband first as you would Jesus, then the Lord is put in control of the home..Peace comes as the wise woman builds an orderly home..I have seen homeschooling moms think that the husband is Mama's helper..No way. . this is not going to work..You have to put your husband first in all that you do.

In the mornings, if Jim had to work later in the day ..he would do his bill paying and organize his checks..Or he had errands to run for the family ..A husband has his own agenda and can't be expected to fit in with Mama's plans at home..No matter what we do, we have to have an orderly home so that the husband can do what he needs to do as head of the home..Even with my writing, I have to fit it in so as not to interrupt my husband..I want to say to Jim. ."Honey, don't ya know I have 100 or so readers that are waiting to read my writing?"? !!! But ya know, Jim ain't Mama's helper..So I fit it in when I can..And this is the anointing on my writing that I obey my husband and honor him as I would Jesus ..You wouldn't' want all of me ..just the anointed part ..And this part is the part that is overshadowed by my husband..And this makes a peaceful home..The scriptures tell my husband: "Give not thy strength to women nor thy ways to which destroy Kings." I have whispered this in Jim's ears often as I have hugged him "Good -Bye " before he has gone to work..A lot of times it was to my own hurt. But I must give up my will and surrender to my place as keeper at home and helper to Jim.

No, the world will think we wives are crazy..so what? They don't love God or want to build a temple for His glory..I am in my house busy and the neighbor women run all day..I am not going to go out and run with them..I am a woman of strength and dignity ..I look well to the ways of our household and I don't eat the bread of idleness ..And the heart of my husband safely trusts in me..Papa and I live in peace and rest most of the time..we live in a happy contentment..But a woman who is always screamin' and belly aching about how she didn't get this and that and she wants this and that and on and on and on? That is a living hell for a man to live in a home like that..And the children end up with all kinds of maladies . . But a peaceful, obedient mother makes a happy home and leads her family to heaven..When things go wrong, she is quiet and she prays and seeks the Lord and she listens to her husband and he leads her..She serves her husband; not as a man pleaser but as a God pleaser..She obeys God with a singleness of eye..

13

Hearts of Submission

Dear Mothers, Ya know, lately the Lord has impressed upon me how much I need to submit to my husband Jim .As we go to new levels in our faith we come into more spiritual wars too. The wives I have known in my life who were very submissive to their husbands were always the most spiritual..Mary L., at age 75, is very submissive to her husband ..And when she prays for ya, you know you have been prayed for..But she is not proud or arrogant ..she is very meek and quiet..And often the women who have been very spiritual but then they walked out on their marriage? They lose their anointing . .And ya know, I had a woman the other day say to me.."Well I won't live like you do.. My husband isn't King of me ..I can do what I want".. Well at the time I wanted to soft soap it..But after I prayed, I thought, "Lord please give me another whack at her and I won't soft soap it the 2nd time.." I mean what does it matter if someone likes it that your husband is King of the home or not? Next time I am gonna say to her, "Yeah my husband is King of our home and I like it like that." I don't have to give her a reason why either..It's a spiritual thing and you can't explain it in a minute or two..And to try will make you look like your biscuits aren't done on one side..But ya know, if I please Jim and I please the Lord, then that's all I care about.. And the Bible says that if your ways please the Lord, then even your enemies will be at peace with you.. And ya know, I don't really give a hoot what the women around me think of me?

There is so much deception out there..On the TODAY show a few mornings ago? They had these women hooraying for the WOMEN'S CONSTRUCTION CONVENTION.. the women looked like they could handle it too..BEASTS OF BURDEN..I thought, man alive, those men who encourage these women to work construction are nothing but slave owners..Sissies who are too lazy to do their own work. .When I was young and in the 1970's, we all knew that a woman had to be very careful of her uterus ..We were cautioned about doing a lot of long distance running, etc. as it could hurt our uterus..Everyone knew that a woman wasn't supposed to lift heavy things as it could displace her womb..Always, we took it easy after child birth for at least two weeks, so that our wombs would pop back into place...Not that we stayed in bed, but we didn't lift a lot or do a lot of work..Mainly, we took care of the baby. .We had few visitors and almost no one held your baby but you or another family member..To run Baby off to Daycare was unthinkable . . And yet now- a- days these poor women are so unprotected and are expected to do construction work? This is barbaric . .If they have a uterus after doing this work then they probably can't have a baby with it..I am speaking generally too..I know some women can squat in the garden ..have the baby ..and come in and eat lunch and go back out .But my womb was displaced for a long time after having 6 children. .I am ok now..But there were times I thought my womb was slipping out . .And I am sure this is why I couldn't have more than 6 children. .But we do need to know that we are the weaker vessels . . And we need to stay in our place as submissive wives and train our men to treat us as weaker vessels by our willingness to submit.

If you want your husband to act more like a man, try being more like a Biblical woman. Like Mary or Sarah and the women in the Bible ..We should not take spiritual authority over our men..Just because we may be more spiritual, this doesn't make us the Priest of the home. . If we submit, and they make mistakes in judgment .. then that is their fault..But if we get in the way and stand between them and God, then the devil will come after us. We need to be quiet and hide off from the world. .We need to blend with our nests and our young ones . .We, as submissive godly wives need to mind our own HOME business and have hearts like a child's heart..

14

Spiritual Housewifery

Dear Mothers, Oh Mercy I was already to write this morning and Rose came to the door. .Oh man, I cried out to God to just give me a break. .But then the Lord impressed me that there was a reason. .So I told Rose what I was writing about on the email. But I have had so many interruptions that I could scream..Rose sure gave me some ideas as to what to write ..But even as I went over here to the email machine, I said to God I just can't be interrupted again or I will have a conniption fit. I wasn't even gonna write. . But ya know, I glanced up at Dixie's picture that I have on my shelf and I just felt like she was calling me out of heaven to write about wisdom.."Tell them about Wisdom Connie, they need it to be strong in the Lord." And yet I feel like I have been run over by a truck to get back here to the E - machine..So to answer Helen ..No Helen I know that you know all about homemaking..But I do want to say that

the homemaking I am trying to explain isn't what you have. .
You have a wonderful homemaking spirit and it is in
submission to your husband and you are where God wants ya.
. . And you don't need what I am writing about. . Definitely
not. As Rose and I sat here this morning, I said to her.."Rose
remember when we would get so down and Dixie would say to
us, "Well you girls need to just get into your homemaking."
And Rose and I would say later as we left Dixie's house.."What
the heck does she think we ARE doing? " I mean Rose and I
worked like Dogs anyway. We would be insulted that Dixie
would say that we needed to be into our homemaking. .So I
reminded Rose of this today as we sat and visited over Coffee. .
See Rose and I get it now. .but we didn't then. . So I said to
Rose, "So how do I explain all of this in words on the email?"
She said, "Well just say what Dixie told us.." But I told Rose
and she sure agreed that Dixie never explained anything. . You
just picked up on it as you were around her. . Dixie would just
say, "Well just get in to your homemaking and it will break the
devil off of the situation." We kept wondering how? And me
being a writer, I had to know things in words. . Well I had to
pray a lot about it and Rose and I finally understood . .

Now here is how Rose does it: Her husband is hands down
the worst guy I have ever known. Mary Lehman called this
morning and we all prayed for Rose on the phone. I held
Rose's hand and cried and cried. I just wept and weep now as I
write. Rose being dry - eyed never understands when I cry for

her. . She is so strong in faith, she doesn't know I am crying for her. When Mary L. called and we prayed for Rose? Mary also cried on the phone. . We just weep in tears for Rose. . I am not using her real name here. . Anyway, Rose's house is the sweetest home you could ever enter. . The angels of God are there because Rose is so obedient to God. . She sets a plate at the head of her table for her husband every evening. Now I would have divorced this pig years ago. I forgive him daily for how he is. . But Rose has mercy on him. . And she is a dear Sister in Christ. . She cooks and cleans for a man who is a known adulterer. . She could not do this unless she had faith in God. . She does her homemaking by faith ..And as she walks in faith, she will see His glory. . Randy does support her and her children. . But he didn't just slip once and commit adultery . . He has been committing it for years and years. . Any man can make a mistake and ask God for forgiveness. . That doesn't make him an adulterer. . But one who practices this is one. . I have no doubt in my mind that he would go to hell even today if he died ..He says he is a Christian. . He knows the word backwards and forwards. . And so does the devil, hu? I have told Rose that I would divorce that guy in a heart beat. She says that she knows she has a right to . .but has chosen to stay with him and pray for him to come back to Christ. Rose is broken in heart and yet is calm as a cucumber..

15

Spiritual Homemaking

But ya know, as Rose and I sat together I said, "Ya know the books we used to read on marriage and homemaking were speaking of a different homemaking than what Dixie tried to teach us. . Most of the books written then, as well as now, discuss homemaking in the framework of an almost perfect family." . .Hey, any wife who has a husband who doesn't come home after work isn't having trouble with her homemaking just because she doesn't have the right schedule. . Or she doesn't have her three bags ready when she cleans: One for the garbage ..one to give away to the Good will, and one to store in the attic. Now that would be hunky- dory for the woman who has a good husband who actually comes home after work. . But the three bags full routine won't work for women with some real problems. . And don't get me wrong, we need the strong families like these women have. They are the example. . . But the powerful homemaking spirit is the one that inspires us to clean and cook and be homemakers for a husband who is wayward. This kind of homemaking is a walk of faith and will bring the husband to the Lord.

Ok, here it is in a nutshell: I Pet 3:1: Likewise ye wives be in subjection to your own husbands that if any obey not the word they will also without the word be won by the actions of the wife...Ok what actions? It's the obedient actions of the wise mother in the home. . What other actions would it be in light of the Bible times, etc.? It is the actions of the wife who is in her homemaking. . You may say, "Hey my husband is a loser and I need to work." Well Darlin' I don't doubt that ..You need the money to run the home . . But I will tell ya one thing: "You need the wisdom of God more than the money. . You have to put the wisdom of God first." . Rose used to work and her husband would quit work and invite friends to live with them and eat their food, etc. But Rose finally learned to put the wisdom first. . . And Hey if you are goin' under anyway, you may as well go home and try doing it all God's way. . Let the guy go belly up. He will learn better next time, hu? He will get hungry and go to work. . And ya know, it isn't money and common sense that will run a home that is broken. . . If Satan is in there hackin' away at the marriage or the kids are on drugs? Then you have some real demonic problems. . .Ain't no household schedule on earth that will help ya out. .But go ahead by faith dear mother and make a home for the family. Begin to speak respectfully concerning your wayward husband. Make sure he has the chair at the head of the table. He is the priest of the home whether you let him be or not. He may be a wicked priest but he is one.. none the less. Rose every evening makes a wonderful meal for her adulterous husband. She told me today, "Ya know Connie, I can't worry over Randy. I have to just trust in God. I can't change him. Only God can. . .and he and his girlfriend will someday get what they deserve. I will not take revenge . .I cannot do anything to them to make them listen . .but God can.." And like Aunt Toot used to say, "Pay Days comin'" But we have to go on in God.

We live in a horrid society right now. Broken homes are the norm. And yet God gives us a remedy. . Submit to your own husband as unto the Lord. Let your good works win your husband to the Lord ..Without a word, dear Mothers and wives, be obedient to God as Keepers at Home. . Dear wives of wayward husbands, you are called as a keeper at home just as much as the wife with the good husband. . Do your homemaking as unto the Lord . . Not as a man pleaser but one who pleases the Lord.

Serve the Lord with a singleness of eye.. Put God first and be obedient to your place and calling as Keeper at Home. . Get your faith built up so that you can believe God for your husband. . And then make a glorious home for your family . . a Christian home built on the foundations of faith and visions given to you by God in your prayer chambers...

16

Women Drivers

Dear Mothers, Yesterday someone asked me to write about how I get along without a driver's license . . Well, when the children were all home, we almost never went to a Doctor . . If we went, it was an emergency . . But to have regular appointments to go to ..check ups and all? We just never did all of that. I used the home remedies and we never ate a bunch of junk food. So for emergencies, Jim took the kids to the hospital or whatever...Now I realize that for some of you, that wouldn't work. And then to go to the grocery store, I would just go once a week and Jim took me. . I know how to drive and all. But I just decided that I didn't want folks to expect me to run here and there. And if you can just tell someone, "I don't have a car as my husband is at work," then that cuts out a lot of explaining..

We live in a society of women that get up in the morning and hit the bricks as a habit. And if you drive and have a 2nd car, then they expect you to get out there and run too. Sure we can out and out tell them. . "Hey I can't do that, I have to stay home and dust." But they don't understand that. And they are insulted..!!! And some women have one emergency after the other and want you to help them. Well they have all the "Emergencies" because they want to run all the time and won't stay home and mind their own business. They wanna run and they want you to run with them. .one way or the other. . Even if they have to fall off the roof to get you to take them to the hospital to get you out of the house. . But if you have your husband as the head of the car.. and if someone needs something like a ride some place? Then they have to go through the husband. If I had a license when my older children were in their teens, I never could have homeschooled the little kids. I mean older teens will try to work their Mother while the Dad is gone. . But if the children know that the car is gone and we are home for the day, then it helps them to settle down. . Danny was such a little character to homeschool anyway . . He was so full of energy . .He was easily distracted. He was always worried about the holidays and what we were all gonna do. And who was coming home for Thanksgiving and Christmas. . And with children of so many ages, I had to have order in our home to homeschool. .We went on field trips like maybe twice a year. . And we went to the homeschool roller skating once a month. .But mainly we stayed at home and did school. .I didn't have visitors during homeschool days ..I did our school in the mornings and then around 1:00 in the afternoon I was done. So then if their certified teacher had to come or whoever, I did all of this in the late afternoon. But for children to learn, it has to be quiet and orderly. .

   I still don't drive or have a license. My relatives would keep me goin' all day and night. My not driving forces me into my home duties and seems to keep order in the folks around me. And with a second driver, you have to have more car insurance ..And the upkeep of 2 cars is hard ..And mercy if ya don't need a 2nd car for something important, then why have it? If you are a stay at home Mother, then why don't you stay home? I have seen many Mothers who can't homeschool as they can't stay home. .They just can't !!! They have itchy feet and have to be on the move. .And it is destroying their homes..And isn't it insulting to the husband? I mean he is workin' like a dog to keep the family afloat and his wife is out running carefree all day? Wasting gas and money. .That sure is not praising or honoring your husband as the priest of the home. .It shows him no respect at all. . And folks say to me, "Well the kids are grown. What do you do all day? " Well I have plenty to do ..with Papa and Baby Rose..

17

Hand-Made Homes

Dear Mothers, Well I don't know about you all, but I am stayin' in my homemaking. . The Lord is on me like a hen on a bug to stay writing like I have been. . I am keeping my mind on canning and cooking and preparing my home for winter. .We as home makers need to choose our battles . And I choose the works of my hands and the battles to get the food I need for winter. . and store it...I choose the work of homemaking. . I choose to mind my business here with Papa. . And the Bible says in Deut. 28, that if I am obedient, I will be blessed. .Well the Lord has called us to be obedient in the area of keepers at home. . As we tend our gardens and work with our hands to make a home? I think this takes us to the inner court. See we battle to enter our rest as homemakers. .We battle worry and fears to come into our rest. .Our homemaking is the fruit of our battles that have been won. .All summer I battled fears and worry over my kids. .Now they are at peace and I am too. .So I can come to the inner court of my temple. .I can hide away in my secret garden. .I can build my house up and make a place to honor the Lord. .The meek and quiet spirit is the spirit that is submitted to our husbands. .it is the spirit that is at peace. . If you are fearful and upset, it is because you don't have a meek and quiet spirit. .You are not submitted to your husband or to the Lord. . We cannot cook and can or keep house if we are so worried and upset and looking out the window like antsy cats on hot tin roofs. .No we must give our burdens to the Lord . .We must seek peace and ensue it. .If we have food and covering, we must be content. A Mother who is content and peaceful can make a home. .But we must keep our minds on the work of the Lord set before us.

Every wise woman builds up her home, but the foolish tear it down with their hands. We must not be busy- bodies running from house to house tattling and speaking things we shouldn't speak. .No, our lives must be at home.. Our lives must center around "Our Home" .."Our own Business." Yes, at times God may call us out to do something for someone. .But generally our work is at home ..on the homestead. A homestead just means the place where you have your home. .Ours is called, "The Hultquist Homestead." But we shouldn't want to run off the area God has called us to tend. .I live in the city but I have a big back yard. So this is my little farm. .This is my working farm. .and I am glad to be here ..Satan wants to interrupt my peace and yours but let's not let him. .Let's just stay out of his way . Let's just humble ourselves under the mighty hand of God. .Let's take that lower door that you must bow before you enter. .Let's put on our coverings of spiritual housewifery. . Let's put on our capes of humility and shod our feet with the gospel of peace. Let's say with our mouths and confess to the world. ."My husband is my priest and I submit to him. .His heart safely trusts in me and he has no need of spoil." [Spoil, meaning drugs or alcohol or other women or whatever.] We are to satisfy our husbands in every way we know how.

The Lord isn't out there looking for a woman with all the answers to every theological question. .He longs to see Mother at home who lives in peace with her children. .She is wise and obedient and dutiful and quiet. .Her hands are busy. Her mind is stayed upon God. God is calling His daughters to come to Him. Are you His daughter, the Kings Daughter? Are you all glorious within? Or are you full of fear and worry and unable to get your kitchens ready for the winter? Are you a love slave or a slave to fear and worry...Check your inward adornment of the Spirit. .Is it meek and quiet? Choose your battles ..will it be your own business or the business of the neighbors or someone else's..

18

Mother, the Star of the Home

Dear Mothers, I am up early and Papa had an errand to run so I have a bit of time to write. He has to work later so I could write later but I get so many interruptions if I don't write early in the day. Ya know, one of the things the Lord keeps telling me is that we need to live our lives for eternity's sake? I mean if we live for ourselves then when we die, then whoever we are dies with us. But as Christian Mothers, we need to live our lives to be remembered. As we homeschool our children, we teach them things that will be taught to their children...You know, often I feel like I am like Laura in the "Little House on the Prairie" books. She was the writer and wrote about the folks she admired. .Ma Ingalls was the Star in most of her writings. Ma Ingalls was the Star of the Home. .Her husband, Charles, had itchy feet and was such a trail blazer. .God made him like that. .But Ma. .she never missed a shot. She was a woman of strength and dignity. No matter where she had to live, even if it was in a sod hut underground, Ma made a home. And she made supper and she washed the dishes and put them away after each meal. .And her daughters had to sit up straight and use their best manners even if it was just them and their Mother sitting on a log . .Their dignity was inside them and poverty, or what others thought could not be driven out of their souls. .Ma Ingalls was Ma Ingalls in a dug out made of grass or in a palace. She would have remained the same. .Our strength and dignity doesn't depend upon our money . .it depends upon our character and who we are in God. .And when our character is tested in the hottest of fires and we cry out, "Lord don't you care that I perish?" It is there that our gifts and fruits of the Spirit are being pruned ..The fire becomes so hot and the flesh is burned off. .And we come out glistening ..shining with His Glorious Holy Spirit. .Meet for the Masters use with gifts of the Spirit that will endure forever. He creates us in His image ..Our righteousness is but filthy rags . . Only He and His words will endure forever in us.. May our families remember us as Christian Mothers. .Mothers who were easily entreated . .Mothers who loved them when no one else did. .Mothers who are courageous enough to go on and stand with God in the midst of Satan's heckles and jeers. . Having done all to stand; we stand with our faith bright . .our visions crisp ..Our anointing glistening, we stand. .Our hair wet with the oil of the Holy Spirit, we stand in Him..Stars. .

everlasting stars of the home.. Soldiers who refuse to give up, to quit, or lose the battle...

19

Being a Homemaker

Dear Mothers, It's early in the morning, 4:30 a.m. I feel rested as I went to bed early last night. .I have straightened up the house and decided what to fix for Jim's breakfast before he goes to work mid -morning. He asked for sausage and eggs and I think I will make muffins too. .I love to make muffins as they are so easy to stir up ..You don't have to get out the mixer or do anything special but just stir up some batter. I enjoy stirring things in a bowl. . Also I enjoy making gravy because all you do is stand and stir...You aren't running about doing a hundred things at once like we Mothers are known for. .Yes . .in the quiet of an evening I love to stand and stir Papa's gravy. . . Ya know, about 2 years ago I was looking for some nice deep crock bowls to mix things in . .And I just couldn't find any that I liked. I did finally find some at the Dollar Store. .Jimmy's {our son who is 37} wife, Aleks, loves to cook and mix things up in a bowl and she just loves my bowls. .they are a steel blue color and are deep . .I have 4 going from the big one to a small one. The biggest one I use to mix up bread in and I knead it mostly in the bowl. .The crock holds the heat in and makes the yeast very happy. .Then the next smallest bowl, I mix muffins in and I have a certain spoon that I use to mix them. .The spoon fits perfectly and you can get some good leverage to stir. . . I like to hear my spoon and bowl make a clop- clop hollow sound when I stir up muffins.. This way I know that the eggs are getting mixed in and some air to make them rise good. You don't want to beat muffins but just sort of get all of the ingredients mixed up. .You don't want flour chunks in it though, so make sure it is mixed up good. But don't beat it like you would a cake. .And the best secret I know to making good quick breads is to be sure to preheat your oven and make sure it is good and hot. Ya know, when I was a young married wife at home, I always had an electric mixer. But some of my friends just starting out didn't have one. Jill R. never used an electric mixer.. She just stirred everything up by hand. It took her awhile but she got it done. .

Jill was so poor. .but did such a good job raising her children alone. .Her children loved chocolate chip cookies. .And she would get a pkg. of choc chips and make them last for months. . . Sometimes she would make choc chip cookies with one choc chip on the top of each cookie. .And as long as there was one choc chip on the top of each cookie, then her children thought they were choc chip cookies and that was good enough for them. They were happy. Jill had such a powerful homemaking spirit. .She moved into this old farm house. .Well the back door wouldn't close because the back part of the house was sagging. So she propped up the back corner of the house with wood and rocks and hoisted it up and then she could close the door. .And that house could be in a magazine; it is so artistically done. It is absolutely charming. .We girls always loved that poor but squeaky clean look? That look of frugality that carries with it a look of honesty and hard work. Well so many of us were poor and had to make a home with this and that.. We had no choice but to choose the look of poor but honest. Jill's home was always a quiet country charm ..a place for everything and everything in its place. .My home was always straight up Hillbilly ..I always wanted my home to look like Jill's ..But Jill didn't have 4 boys hangin' off the roof ..Or lighting paper airplanes on fire and throwing them out the window. .And she didn't have Papa who can't figure out what all these doo- dads are for. ."And why do you have a candle on? It's day light?" But ya know, Dixie and I and Jill we were so poor. .And when we would go to each other's house we would look around our house to find something to bring to the other friend to make her day go better; To ease her heavy load.

20

A Keeper at Home

But ya know? Shoot, we young Moms back in my day? We
thought we were doin' good to get through the day. .We didn't
have a bread machine to make our bread. I know when I wrote
about making my bread with just a spoon and a bowl . .one of
the ladies on my old list thought I was being a smarty pants.
She didn't believe me. .But I mean that's how I make bread
..And I just use leftovers to make it. If I have a couple cups of
juice that no one is drinking up, I just use it for the liquid for
my bread. .Or water I cooked vegetables in? Whatever.. And if
I am in a big hurry and don't want to get flour on my table, I
will just knead my bread in my big crock kneading bowl. But
you don't need a lot of new stuff to make a home for your
family. You have the Lord God and He is your provider. As
long as you have a roof over your head and a place to cook . .
And a place to bed your children down at night in a safe and

clean warm place, then you are living good. I went to this little Tea Shop here in my town. .and I just loved it. .Nothing that woman had on her tables matched. . NOTHING . . .She had cloth place mats from the 80's. .China ware from the 50's. . glass goblets from the 60's. .un- matching silverware. The tablecloth matched with nothing else. .I loved it!! This woman was very creative and this was her style.. Now a lesser woman couldn't have carried this off.

But ya know, we Mothers back in the 70's, we didn't have much but we had some guts? Some Moxie? That it takes to raise a family? See I was mostly alone raising my 3 children for the first 12 yrs of my marriage. So Jill would take me to the store. Her car had windows that she propped up in the winter and they fell down slowly, and by summer they were all down. . .Well we all looked good . . like we knew what we were doin' as long as it didn't rain. . But when it would rain, we would ride in that car with dignity anyway .. And if someone would come over and talk to me on the passenger side, I would act like I wasn't all wet. .Or I would act like I liked the rain and the fresh air.. Jill and I "B.S.- ed" so many people with makin' them think we were ok. . I mean women who had much more than we did, asked us to pray for them. .We always had women following us all over asking us to pray for them. .And our kids were the same way. .They made all of their friends envy them. . And yet we were so poor, but we didn't confess it or let it take us down. . Christian Joy {Daughter 30} is a takeoff of all of this. .When she first went to NYC, she would go to the

Salvation Army and buy old prom dresses and fix them up and sell them for hundreds of dollars...

But ya know, rich or poor, a woman of dignity is a woman of dignity. .And she will make a home one way or the other for her children if she has even the barest of necessities . .If she has a husband or not ..or if he is a good man or an alcoholic or drug abuser? A wise woman will not let anyone take her down or take her strength. .And it takes some Moxie to submit to a husband you don't agree with. .A lesser woman can't submit because she is very weak in herself and can't stand up for God. .. A weak woman will look after herself because she can't handle anymore than that. .A woman of strong moral courage will make a home and submit to her husband. .And she will carry it off with strength and dignity. She is not afraid and she will be brave in adversity. And if she has to stand alone, then so be it. .She will be lonely and feel hurt inside..And yet she won't sin against God or her family by hangin' around women who don't care about their families. .Ya know, Christian Joy and I were talking on the phone lately.. She lives in NYC and we were talking about the demonstrations goin' on there. .She said, "Mom something has to give one way or the other.." She said, "Ya know Mom, it's coming down to where folks are gonna have to know how to make it on their own ..Us kids know how to make it because of our teachings at home."

21

The Suffering Saints

Now -a -days, you see these Christians running around spouting from the pulpit the 10 steps to success. .or whatever.{meaning the 10 steps to getting rich in this world system}. .I turned on the TV last week and came across this lady preacher. I needed a good laugh? I watched her a minute. . . She says, "Everyone raise your hand if you love money and want some.." Well the poor schnooks all raised their hands.. She said, "Well sure we all love money" She said that was just being honest. .But you know what I spoke up and talked to the TV and said?: "I don't love money. " My own daughter Christian told me "Mom too much money ruins your creativity". .I am for that thinking. .I told Jim the other day that what I needed, money couldn't buy. .Well we expect the poor lost souls in the world to think of money as a god. .But this thinking has invaded the Christian church. .It's like if you are poor then it is your own fault and if ya had any horse sense, you would be downright ashamed of yourself. .Well any Christian who has it made in the shade is gonna be happy {in a way} . The trick, Darlin', is to be happy with what ya got. .To somehow cultivate the love of Christ in your home even though you have barely enough to feed the family. .

There is this realm of Common sense. .But when the common sense doesn't work anymore, then you have to get into the miracle power of Christ. .Common sense is for folks who have enough money to live on and be common and can live dutifully and prudently with what God has given them. .And we expect them to do so. .They are what keep the rest of us in shoes? We need the Saints with the families who are able to make it. .But some of you Mothers are like Monica. .You get one hole in the boat plugged up and another one comes loose ..You are always building the spiritual house and trying to hold it up as you fix supper with your foot.. You wish you could be perfect and yet you are always doing a dozen things half way. . You are overloaded and over stressed ..and always running to catch up. .You wish you had a home like the Charity tapes advertise. .well I wish I had a home like this. .you bet. .But ya know, even though Jim is a believer he ain't no Dr. Dobson? Poor Dr. Dobson would choke to death in my house. .The cigarette smoke alone would kill him. He wouldn't even come to my house in the first place. .And Dr. Dobson is Dr. Dobson and I love to hear him talk on TV. .But that is probably the closest I will ever get to him.. And now what would the worldly church of today think of Mother Monica? And more importantly what would Mother Monica think of the church today? Well hopefully she would have a sense of humor about it, because if she didn't laugh, she would cry her heart out...and be crushed beyond repair. The only thing that keeps me half the time is my sense of humor. .

Last week I knew Annie was havin' a hard time.. Well I made a lot of jokes on the email to cheer her up. .I know sometimes I get "out there"? But I will go for the lady with the most grief and play the Lord's court jester. .I get misunderstood . .But ya know I could give a dang? If I can keep Annie peddling her bike, I feel like I will keep the rest of ya goin' . .I will risk being misunderstood? I do this a lot to reach the Mother on the group that is the furthest down? I know some of you feel like you get a pie in the face once in awhile . .Well I wasn't aiming for you ..it's just that there is some real heartache that goes on with this group. .There are many Mother Monicas represented here. .And unlike other email groups, I am not going to make the Monicas feel like 2nd class citizens of Heaven because their husbands don't go to church and sit up straight when the Pastor walks by. .We as wives and mothers are to be dutiful Christians .We have Christian homes if we ourselves are Christians. .The angels and God's Holy Spirit are with us.

22

Love Slaves (Part 1 of 3)

Dear Housewives, Oh glory to God... I have a vision in my heart to share.. This morning as Jim and Dan went off to work and I told them Good-bye... I love you. . the door shut and a vision came.. . I saw the daughters of Israel dancing before the Lord.. They had head coverings and long skirts and aprons and bare feet.. They were dancing before the Lord with all of their might... they were casting out idols and the gods of feminism... they were celebrating womanhood and motherhood and wifehood. . they were declaring to Satan, 'You no longer have us bound in chains of oppression... We are women. . Child bearers. . True Women made for true men of God. . We are women and glad to have a man to want us and love us. We love our own husbands and submit as wise servants of Christ'.. ..I see women who will wear aprons just to make the enemy mad..

They will get up in the morning and RUN to put on an apron... Some will make aprons as a cottage business.. and many women of God will buy them and learn to make their own.. Oh revival is coming to the house of God.. Daughters of a new Revolution... Women with mighty men of courage to cover them and wives who will submit to Christ and to the leading of their husbands.. Women who would be ashamed to say, "My husband is not a man of God" ... Women ashamed to say, "I am barren"... These women are prayer warriors.. that pray as if their lives depend on it.. because it does.. Women who would be ashamed to say " I work outside the home because I hate my job as a homemaker.." Women who take off their shoes and throw them in the air as a symbol of liberation.. These women declare.. "I'm not going anywhere .. my work is here and no one .. not Satan or all the demons in hell can make me leave or turn tail and run... I have been redeemed .. I am a woman .. a keeper at home and no demon in hell is gonna move me off the path God has chosen for me to walk"..

So now, what will we do with all these women who claim the Lord in their 3- piece black suits and brief cases? These women are the slaves among us.. we need to rescue them and help them back to reality.. Their husbands sneer at them behind their backs.. and dishonor them in their hearts.. .. Lazy men send these women off to work and to bring home the money ... all the time telling them that they are worth more than a housewife... These men keep their wives barren so that she can earn more money.. and when she is old, they find a new model and she is left without children to comfort her in her old age... Who is the slave here to man? These women have bought a lie that says unless I ignore my female self, I can't express myself.. In other words they are saying ... I am not worth anything .. because I was born a woman. .I must ignore my female side in order to become somebody. These poor women followed the crowd and bought a lie... a lie of death .. the death of their own children .. All for the desire to have wealth here on earth .. they have missed the treasures of heaven. Women who submit to many men .. because they choose not to submit to one man -their husbands...

23

Feminist Slaves (Part 2 of 3)

Dear Hearts, I am not saying hateful things to feminists... I love them .. My heart breaks for them.. I had a dear friend who was one. She had bought the lie.. She was very submissive to her husband but wanted to work. Her husband expected her to keep the house clean and work too.. Also to do errands after she got off work.. take back library books ... look for new ones.. run after prescriptions . .pay bills.. etc. She went to work before the sun was up and got home when the sun went down. She and her husband had discussed her staying home and being a full time homemaker.. it almost happened too. Then she got laid off from her job... She drew unemployment... all day long she talked on the phone, watched TV, and gained weight.. So did her husband think she should do this full time? Of course not.. So he insisted that she work and she wanted to work.. As time went on, she got clearer and clearer on the truth of this whole deal and again decided she wanted to stay home .. Her husband was more stubborn than ever about it. So she tried to work at her outside job and be a full time homemaker at the same time.. she made homemade pies every week .. his favorite, and homemade noodles, and you name it... this woman certainly went the extra mile and then some...I knew her very personally .. and I know she gave it her best shot... I hate to say what happened in the end...She never succeeded, let's put it that way.. I don't blame her or her husband... Feminism is out there and it has many slaves.... .We women of God who are to teach by our Godly behavior are sorely teaching our men the wrong message... and we are reaping strongholds of misery.. But these strongholds can be broken ... are being broken .. the truth sets the captive free...I really feel like a pansy . .some of you ladies are catching this quicker than I am..

Many of you young women see through feminism as it has clearly hurt your lives.. as you are the product of mothers who were feminists. I was brought up in the 1950's and it was just starting then... But as I have said before, when the church world gets away from the family as being the main structure of Christiandom...then deception comes in and every evil work. . Jesus is our Savior and our Priest and we must know Him as Savior to enter eternal life.. But how do we walk afterwards? The Bible is clear that we are to walk in family order. The only teaching a woman is commanded in the word to teach is the teachings on the home structure.. or to teach children. Titus2:3 says that the older women should live holy lives and sound in faith.. Verse 4 says, so that they can teach the young women to be sober and to love their husbands .. and their children ..Verse 5, To be discreet, chaste, keepers at home, good obedient to their own husbands ... That the word be not blasphemed.. Well the word of God has been blasphemed in Christiandom...Women who have not claimed to know Christ are not at fault... No I don't blame them.. It is the fault of the women of God who have the Lord Jesus Christ. The women at church are on birth control ...If the salt of the earth is on birth control and has no respect for human life .. then why wouldn't the unbelievers get abortions? Babies are being murdered and sold for body parts.. not just a few .. One point 5 million a year.. ? Hello? Stay tuned for part 3.

24

Boy Preachers (Part 3 of 3)

Dear Saints, I'm back .. I was writing about aborted babies. Babies who have been killed because of the lies going on in the church.. What if Mary had been on Birth control? She was a Christian... Feminism teaches us that our wombs are useless and easily removed .. and that the fruit of our wombs are useless too. Here we are the descendants of Abraham, and our mother of faith is Sarah... Here we are women of God who are to carry a godly seed and raise children for Christ.. We are promised as our Godly heritage.. Land Seed, and blessing.... We don't want the land .. we kill the godly seed and we think that the blessing is to kill the godly seed, and that money means we are prosperous...If a preacher stood up and preached against feminism, he would lose half his money... because all the women would quit their jobs and go home and have babies.

You Christian feminists have been scammed good. You are killing your own family ..eating your own flesh. You have sacrificed your children on the altar of the god of money and pride and vanity. You have sold your life for a new car.. Please cast down this god of money .. ask the Lord to forgive you this day.. stomp out this idol in your home in Jesus' name. You say, "Well I need to keep my job to pay for health insurance..." In other words, You need to stay in Egypt because you are afraid to leave...Cast down that idol of fear and get your dancin' shoes on and shout, "Glory." Go back to the Land and eat from the land and use herbs for medicine... Cast down vain imaginations and everything that exalts itself above God. Did Mary and Elizabeth or Hannah go get a hold of the world when they got sick, or their families?? Cast that idol out in Jesus' name... And aren't you ladies sick of being hood winked? By boy preachers who care more for their comfort than your life? And your baby's life? He preaches how to get rich in this present world...Give your money to him and the Lord will bless you and make you rich... I don't know about you all, but I am more than ready to be poor if that's what it takes... Years ago, I used to get up early in the morning and think I needed to watch P.T.L. on TV. Jim would be in a dead sleep when I got up.. but he would be awakened by the Lord and would get up in his sleep and turn that thing off. I sent Tammy 5 bucks ..which I am sure didn't even pay for her mascara. I am so embarrassed to tell that story. . That I actually went behind Jim's back to help Tammy ... But I was young and didn't know any better. But now that I know better, I have changed my ways. If your church teaches good things, then Praise the

Lord... But if they don't? Don't be afraid to cast that idol of religion down and stomp on it... They kicked Jesus out and the church world killed Him... Don't be afraid to stand alone and worship the Lord as your personal Savior.

Most of Christiandom is packed full of teaching.. Many of you mothers are well taught and can easily go out on your own. I have seen so many families healed as they have gotten out of the dead church. Many of you need to come to grips with yourself and decide who you are in Christ. .Are you gutsy enough to stand alone? Cast down these idols and declare openly that you will not worship at Satan's table.. Come out from among them and be separated unto God. I know I teach hard things... and I certainly don't mean go over your husband's head...

25

Our Heat Bill

Dear ladies... Well throw me over Niagara Falls in a barrel.. I feel like I would land on my feet. Guess what? Our heat bill for January was over 500 dollars... for Feb over 300 and for this month guess how much??? Drum roll please....Ladies it was 25 dollars and 87 cents....We used our kerosene burner and spent 40 bucks a month on the fuel....So we saved hundreds on our heating bill. What a gas... I told wild man this morning as we were gloating and pouring coffee .. Baby we've got Moxie!!! Or guts, in other words. Papa kind of laughs and watches me out of the corner of his eye... Like, "Well she thinks she is a pioneer woman now."...I love it that I can smile at the gas company in my imagination and say, "Well you nearly destroyed us financially .. but you didn't make it." I told Jim, "And honey I can save us a lot on water and even more on gas this summer when I use my wringer washer and hang all of our clothes on the line. ".. Oh, I can't wait. Well it is all the Lord and He is the one to get the glory.. but bare with me as I am so proud of my ornery little self. .For the past few months I wouldn't allow the kids to turn up the heat. .I dressed in long underwear.. 2 pairs of socks and jogging clothes over the top.. plus a jumper jean dress over that... and sometimes a jacket over that... On our bed, we used a big comforter and 2 regular blankets.. and flannel sheets... plus we wore the jogging pants and all of our clothes to bed. .At night I covered up my head to keep my face warm. We all did this...Mary and Dan too. And Jim. But the kids are older so we could do this .. I wouldn't have done this if the children were young.... But Mary is 15 and Dan is 18 so they could take the cold. None of us got sick and really we have to say we feel better than we ever have health-wise.

In the mornings, when I would write here with you ladies, after Jim had gone to work? I would turn the kerosene burner off ..so there was no heat on at all, for about 45 minutes . Then when Mary would get up I would turn it back on to have devotions in the living room... I would make it warm and cozy for Mary. Well our dog wanted me to turn the burner on for her and she would cry and stand by the burner while I was typing on the email machine. I feel so proud of my naughty little self that my dog cried for the heat and I didn't.... . And my dog sleeps on the porch at night so she is used to the cold. It was sort of embarrassing to have your outside dog shivering in the corner when company came. Our dog is so happy spring is almost here. Well Papa just went out the door to pay his gas bill with a big grin on his face... I am supposed to be making chili. But instead I am here braggin'...Please forgive this old woman in her glory. But the Lord has given me confidence and I needed it too. I just feel like the little red hen who, when the fox caught her in his bag... she was prepared. She had her little sewing scissors in her apron pocket. .and she cut her way out of the bag and saved her little self.

Our heating bill would have pushed me out the door to work. . . we were in dire straits.. Jim didn't want me to babysit...I was between a rock and a hard place... but the Lord took us through. Jim's Heat bill on budget was going to be $$$ 250.00$$$ a month. That is over our heads. But because our bill was so low this month they put it down and it will be reviewed again in May. And go down further. I just Praise the Lord for His redeeming power and His miracles.

26

Mother's Home Journal

Dear Ladies, Yesterday it was starting to get warmer out. It got to about 60 degrees...It was great. I went out and planted some lettuce up by the house. .also spinach and some other greens. Then I took some pots and planted cauliflower and broccoli and put them close up by the house on the south side. In Iowa, we could safely get another snowstorm before spring. So I am not starting my big garden yet. I have a big wooden table right outside my dining room door. So yesterday, I gathered my clay pots up and filled each with potting soil and then planted herbs in them. I planted black colhash and St. Johns Wart. Also Angelica and lavender. I had a pkg. of lemon-balm seeds so I planted them in a pot to give away as a gift to a friend. .. I have lemon-balm a plenty in my yard.. and it will come up again this spring. It is great in iced tea in the summer. I just stick it in the tea after I have rolled some leaves up tight and released the oil. Just fresh leaves, you don't boil it, just throw it in. Anyway, I put the potted herbs in a box and brought them inside. The weather is too cold this morning for herbs ... It's probably back down to 40 this morning. I will just bring them out when it is warm .. until it stays warm and I can leave them out in the sunshine. I loved going barefoot outside and feeling the soil beneath my feet. When Papa got home from work, I was resting in his chair holding my hands away from the chair as they were black with dirt. He looked at me as if to say... "It's spring." . Praise the Lord. I brought him out and showed him what I had been doing and then he started to pull some weeds away from our apple tree... I went down and looked at the rhubarb and it isn't even starting to come up. .it's still really early Spring here.

My heart is so full of emotion this morning...I long to see my old fashioned sister roses bloom. I pull close to the kerosene burner as if I am afraid to let go of it and embrace spring. I had to be very diligent with watching the burner and conserving heat ...Can I let go of that burden now and go on to a glorious time of spring? How many times adversity has blown hard upon us.. and God has brought us through? I never even realize, at times, that I am under His marvelous grace until He has set me safely upon the shore...Some people laughed at us because we only used 25 bucks worth of gas heat in one month. "Why did you pull a stunt like that?" .. It wasn't a stunt... It's called survival?? Hello?

Today I plan to fix up my window sills for spring. .. I have some little clay pots and I will plant seeds in them ... just to watch them grow. I put plastic wrap over the tops of my seeded pots to keep the moisture in. Probably today I will plant poppies and some other flowers in the little window sill pots. Cucumbers.. I can never get them to grow in pots... I just plant them from seeds when the ground is warm and stays warm. Also Basil ...it has to be warm and stay warm for basil to grow for me. One more item and then I have to get Mary up for school. Last year I bought these garlic seeds. They looked like a little head of white popcorn. I planted the seeds last fall and they are now coming up...Anyone know about these garlic seeds? Usually I plant bulbs. .well I have seen seeds ..but these are like little kernels...

27

Little House and Ma (Part 1)

Every morning after Mary and I have devotions, we watch
LITTLE HOUSE ON THE PRAIRE...Then she starts school.....
We visit and drink coffee or juice while it is on. It is a special
time for us to be together. We talk about how pretty and sweet
Ma is and how brave Pa is. We love it. When Mary was little,
we read all of the Little House on the Prairie books. We have
read a lot of books about Laura, the writer of these books.
There is so much wisdom in those books. Mercy, I needed
Laura's writings, especially when raising the little ones.
Actually the star of the show is Ma. And in Laura's writings,
Ma was the silver thread that wove wisdom and stability
throughout Laura's books.... Laura's only daughter Rose was
sort of a women's libber. Laura respected her mother.. but was
never like her. Ma was so full of wisdom .. and it didn't matter
what Pa did; Caroline ..Ma. . made do. In one story in the
book, Caroline had just planted her garden in the spring and
Pa got itchy feet and wanted to move the family .. Caroline just

got packed and they left.. leaving her garden. In one story, Pa sold the milk cow... and Caroline just said, "Well there goes the milk..." Like, so what? She just trusted Pa .. no matter what. But you could tell in Laura's writings that she sort of resented the fact that Ma never really spoke her mind. After Laura married and set up housekeeping.. she really ruled the roost at times... but it seems her life with her husband, for the most part, was one struggle after the next. She had a lot more material things .... but was far less thankful or content than her Mother was.

Ma was certainly the virtuous woman and never seemed to miss a step...I love watching Ma on the TV series and reading about her. Rose... Laura's daughter, was a famous writer in her day and made a good wage at it... But Laura's writings really endured the test of time. Rose really encouraged Laura to publish her writings. So.. Praise the Lord for Rose....But Ma, who never wrote much of anything, lived such a life of service that she never even needed to write anything... She just lived it and 2 generations of writers recorded it. And now 3 generations or more have come and gone.. I think Rose died in the 1960's... alone and divorced.. no children...She was a bright star that fizzled out.. and would have been forgotten if it were not for Laura and Ma....She had all the gold and worldly things.. But Ma had the life to send out, and her life has touched me in my heart and soul. . Down through the ages.. Ma just lived a loyal and faithful life.. She honored Pa and raised her children to know Christ. She followed Pa wherever

he went. .she just never gave up. .and her life was, and is, a
sermon for we ladies today. She was like Mary, Jesus'
mother,.. she was faithful to her calling...

28

Little House and Ma (Part 2)

Dear Ladies, After I wrote that first part.. .. I wept so. The
Lord has touched my heart so much concerning Caroline
Ingalls..Ma, on Little House on the Prairie. It's early morning
here and the children are still asleep. ... Jim is off to work.
After I wrote, I took a towel and cried into it to muffle the
sounds...so I wouldn't wake anyone up.. Something within me
just poured out in sobs. I ask myself, "Do I want to be a Laura
Ingalls Wilder or do I want to be a Caroline Ingalls? " Well I
am a writer so I have to write...But oh, may God teach me to be
a Caroline...I pray that my life will be the example ...an
example that will live on long after I am dead and gone.

Money is not a measure of success.. and we don't need more
money to preach the gospel .. we need an honest life .. a life
that preaches the gospel. .God will spread the word.. if our
lives say anything at all. Job was a righteous man and the Lord
made sure that even the devil knew that God was proud of Job.
I feel so sober this morning as if the Lord is shedding a light on

my soul. He is looking into my heart. Is there anything in there that He can use. Have my testings and trials produced anything that the Lord can use? I see Him inside my heart seeking my obedience. I see Him now as I write... The room is like a small cave.. a warm light flickers and then burns warmly in the shadows.. He is seeking me...He is pondering things in His heart concerning me. He speaks to His companions, the angels.. " Connie loves me and wants to honor me but is she ready to be used as I have designed? " I feel the Lord's eyes upon me. . .studying my spirit... "Can I trust her?".. He seems to say.

Oh ladies, what else matters except that we would obey Him as Keepers at Home. .that we would submit to our husbands and live lives that are pleasing to God. The world may tell you, "Oh you ain't nothin' . . so what, you had a baby and now you gotta take care of it." Well isn't that all that Mary, Jesus' mother, did? Or Sarah or Elizabeth??? Who cares what the world thinks of us? If you want to be a friend to the world .. you can never be the Lord's friend.. He can't trust you. Oh ladies, when we least expect it the Lord uses us for His glory. We are not God and we don't know what He is doing at times .. we just have to obey His word. Don't look outside your door for the Lord.. look in your heart. Your world will end some day ...did your life count enough on this earth that someone would want to write about it.. other than you?

As believers, we live with one foot in the world and one in heaven. When we lift our foot from this world and put our weight on heaven we make a mark in this world...oh, we hate trials ..but they make such heavy footprints.. if we put all of our weight in heaven, when they come......Our footprints are to lead others to Him.. This hog wash of feminism ..it's a star that has burned brightly and will fizzle out ..and nothing will be left except children crying in the streets.. and souls dying in hell.

Mother should be at home raising children for Christ .Oh ladies, look away from the fame and glory of this present world ...get honest with the Lord.. and be a tool in His hands. Live a life that writers like me would love to write about. And of course in this flock of ladies there are many heroines .. many of you are such examples to me.

29

Homemaking

Dear ladies, As I was trying to write yesterday.. I was talking to Jim, and some of that writing got mixed up... I was trying to make the point that we don't do "faith things" and then shut our faith off to do our homemaking.. No, not all homemaking is spiritual ..but a lot of it is.. The Bible says to yield our members to righteousness.. So If you are praying in faith for the Lord to restore your family? You must then yield your body to the answer to your prayers. You must begin building up your home and preparing your home for a miracle... Learn to make your husband's favorite foods... prepare your whole household to receive the answer to your prayers.. I used to read to the children when they were young, out of the Uncle Arthur devotions for children... The stories often were about walking out your faith.. A family was without food... but the mother was full of faith.. She did as much as she could with the food she had.. But one day they had no food. She didn't lose faith. She just set the table, by faith, and expected a miracle. . . Well they were miles from town and they only went to get their mail about once a month. They sent their son to walk the miles to the post office. . Well in the mail was some money that was owed to the father, for some work he had done and not been paid for. The Lord had spoken to this man to pay his bill .. that he owed to this father in the story. And there are a lot of true stories like that..

I have read many about the women during the depression. Now those were hard times!!!! I really feel that it was the women, mainly, who won that war of poverty. Had those Mothers not made a home in the midst of such an economic storm, where would anyone have rested their souls? The mothers worked hard on their gardens and sewed the clothes for their children. Some made homes in chicken coops.. They just took what they had and went by faith.. The saying, when I was a girl, was always, "A man builds a house but a mother makes a home"..

When I was with the family on Sunday .. Mom was talking about the Depression.. She was saying that when her folks went to buy a farm, they didn't look at the house; They looked at the land.. They made their living from the land.. They were farmers.. The house ... whatever it was ..was up to the mother to make a home out of it. I have seen pictures in old books where the mother wallpapered her house with newspaper... This kept the wind from coming in.. Many children learned to read by reading the wall paper. I read about a woman who had a garden that had dried up during the drought.. well weeds will always grow.. So she canned lambs quarters ..which is what we would call a weed .. But she kept her family going ... How much faith does that take to not give up or lay down.. and instead can lambs quarters? I mean that just makes me ache in my spirit...It makes me want to cry out in intercession for the faith to not give up...Where was this woman at in her faith just before it came to her to can weeds to keep her family in food for the winter? Well we mothers in this age...OOOoooh we face things like that.. just a few of the details have changed.. We don't fight such a war on poverty, as we fight a demonic spiritual war. The women during the Depression did have the example of the older Titus woman.. These women, I think, had more of an understanding of their job as homemaker. .and mother..

30

Breadmaking

Dear ladies, It is Tuesday. .Mondays around here are like stopping a parade after the weekend. I do this because of that.. and that because of this... but nothing on purpose. On Tuesdays I do things on purpose. Today, I will make homemade soup... probably chicken. And hopefully homemade dinner rolls... Papa brought home some bread last night that a friend at work had given to him...It was an expensive pumpernickel brick bread .... Well .. some people may like it... But .. Well, I think it's the day for me to bake bread. I don't follow a recipe for bread.. so get ready for a joy ride as I explain this. First I test my yeast. I put about 2 Tbs. of yeast in a bowl of hot water with a little sugar. . 2 Tbs. is about 2 pkgs. of yeast. When the yeast starts to bubble, then I know the yeast is good .. and also ready to use. Set aside. .. Then I get out my big bread bowl... It's a crock. I start out by adding 2 cups of heated liquid into the bowl. This liquid can be anything... Such as water, milk, fruit juice, tomato juice, leftover potato water, buttermilk - just a liquid...2 cups. Then add your oil for the fat...oil or melted shortening... anywhere from a Tbs. to a cup .. whatever. Sir that up. If you want to add a few eggs at this point go ahead...if you are out of eggs, skip it. If you love eggs add 1 to 3 or so . stir that up. Pour in some sweetener: A Tbs. of sugar or up to a cup. .whatever....Use a cup of honey if you want to. Or use leftover jelly or pancake syrup . . . not too much more liquid, though unless you want to add more yeast, another -Tbs. Or 2 . Then begin adding your flour... Stir it up good until it looks like a cake mix.. beat it up good. Then I add my yeast ... Then carefully, cup for cup, stir in about 6 cups of flour. You will end up with a glob of dough. So now take the glob out, put it on a floured surface and knead it, adding more flour as you go. If your dough turns out soft and easy and sweet, just make dinner rolls with it. If it is more stiff and elastic .. then congratulations - you made bread dough. Let it rise in a warm place, then shape it and let it rise again and then bake it , about 375 degrees for about a half hour? I don't know. I just check mine ...

Now here are some housewife secrets to making really good bread or dinner rolls. . Ladies, ya gotta love it. .. If it turns out wrong, you didn't love it enough... and it helps to wear a long skirt and an apron .. an old fashioned one of your grandmas.. or one you got at a garage sale... and a bandanna on your head. The apron has to be old and look comfortable. It has to be quiet when you make bread. So get the children settled with their toys and games and books. . Tell them everything has to be peaceful... Mama is going to make homemade bread. It helps to have soup simmering on the stove also to create a warm steamy kitchen. Then when you set your bread out to rise on the stove top, the soup keeps the bread warm, friendly and comfortable. Yeast is alive and it likes a warm happy atmosphere. And good homemade.. and handmade bread creates a happy home. Papa always comes to my kitchen after work and starts lifting up lids on pots on the stove. And if he sees bread rising on the stove ..under an old cotton print cloth, it sets his mood for a quiet evening at home. Good bread ... made with willing hands. A happy mother whose aim is to make a quiet and loving nest, always makes GOOD bread.

31

Blessed are the Poor in Spirit (Part 1)

Dear Wives, Last week I got so mad at Jim.. I wanted my way and he wanted his way. And then he got into a BLACK mood and then I got into a blacker one. Well Papa, he is out in the world all day.. and Mama is at home prayin' . .we see things in different lights. My sin is always that I think Jim should feel like I do about things.. He often thinks that I am not respecting him as a man and not honoring him as my husband. .the bread winner .. the head of the house. Jim is very territorial which is a good trait in a man. They like being the head of the house... and they know everything that is going on in the house from top to bottom.. That's Jim... When Mama gets outside that boundary line... and especially when Papa is sick with his sinus problems???. Things go boom. When Papa's mood is black .. it begins to change to gray when he looks at Mama and sees that her mood is changing to black.. Blacker, and then to fire engine black. The Lord spoke to my heart finally as I wrestled in prayer with the whole thing...And then I went to the grocery store.. As I entered the door, the Lord spoke to my heart, "Connie, blessed are the poor in spirit.. be pitiful, be courteous. Connie you are more spiritual than your Jim .. forget your own hurts and love Jim and minister to him." Something really broke within me. And I saw this whole picture as the Lord saw it. God is not interested in who is right.. He looks at our hearts and our desire to please Him.. I pleased the Lord when I forgave. .when I took the lower seat. .when I humbled myself before the Lord and to my husband. It's not who is righteously correct.. It's who is the most humble before God. As I forgave Jim.. I could ask God to forgive me for my vanity and pride. That stiff unholy flesh that needs to be RIGHT? Will be the death of we women if we don't watch out..

I really think it is the year of the women.. Man ALIVE. . . . . . women are just worshipped these days...they seemingly can't do anything wrong. Women can stay home and do nothing to build up the home ... just sit there and be pretty.. and the world would tell her that this is her right.. Let a man try that for a while.. and he is called a snake.. All of this deception lives around we Christian wives and mothers .. and we need to be very careful of it...We are fast losing our places in our homes. If we don't get to work and show our husbands that we are making a difference in the quality of the home by staying home, then they won't want to support us. A wife at home has a definite advantage over her husband in spiritual things. Her husband is really, in a way, sacrificing part of his spiritual life to go out and work for his family.. Well not really .. but in a way... I mean, I am here and very able to grow spiritually ..

Every day I write in the mornings and my spiritual life has grown a lot as I have been faithful to keep writing.. I have noticed that I am so much more clear.. and have so much more discernment than I used to have. So when Jim starts to match wits with me.. I'm liable to blow him into the next state. .With just a look.. And I know that some of you ladies know what I mean....Trouble is, I am not the head of the house.. and God doesn't think I am, just because I am more spiritual. This whole thing is like me bragging that I have a winter coat to wear in the cold and he doesn't.. when he was the one who bought me the coat....

32

Blessed are the Poor in Spirit (Part 2)

Dear Mothers, While the world may tell us that we can do anything.. we better not try that in front of the old man. Pride comes before a fall.. In the world, the woman is told to square her shoulders and stick her chest out and do what she wants.. regardless of what her husband says...Satan is just pulling these women into slavery... No one can just do as they please; I don't care who they are. I think in Christiandom, the biggest sin that women are committing is the sin of pride and unforgiveness.. We have to walk in love and forgiveness.. It doesn't matter who is right.. God's servant among us is the one who will humble herself and be the peacemaker.

Just lately, I faced all of this with my own mother.. Dad is still in the hospital .. Of course I am ranting and raving about the medical help he is NOT getting. .Mother, on the other hand, trusts in doctors. Mom called me 2 nights ago and said the doctor said that Dad could die any minute.. My response was, "Mom why do you believe that stuff?" I was ashamed of myself after I said that.. I couldn't sleep that night hardly at all.. I had drawn my sword of righteousness again and nearly killed someone who didn't understand where I was coming from at all. Mom was hurt and didn't understand that I was laboring in prayer for Dad's life. I may have been Scripturally right... but where was my humility and respect to my mother who was losing her mate of 59 years? I told God that I was sorry.. so sorry.. When I got to the hospital .. I soothed my mother.. I said, "Mom I understand .. you believe the doctors are right.. and I will just agree with you.". See I have to be at peace with my mother... or Dad could never be healed.. We have to walk in forgiveness and love and peace with those around us.. We must go to the level of faith of the weakest one. I came into agreement with Mom that the doctors were doing right with Dad. And if God can use an ass, he can use a doctor... Mom is from the old school.. where the doctors were gods and if they killed you .. Well, they couldn't help it.. As I agree with Mom that the doctors will do what is right.. this helps me in my faith ..to walk in peace .. and know that God can still do a miracle. But I am not going to get a miracle by walking up and over my mother's head..

We must be patient with those around us.. and see their point.. and encourage them where they are at. If they have a little faith and it is in a doctor, then it is faith even if it is misdirected. Maybe God will use my mother's faith in her doctors.. I'm not going to kill her faith because it isn't like mine. I said all of this to say that we need to understand that some of us are given more discernment than others.. But as women, we don't have the authority to take spiritual authority over a man.. We need to drop back out of sight and pray our prayers to the Man in authority {Jesus Christ}, over every demon and every man...

We must be quiet and submissive and loving to those who are poor in spirit. Whether that means your husband or your own folks. Be glad that you understand the Lord.. because you have had the time to spend with Him and know His heart.. But many don't understand Him... We must show the world who He is by our good works.. I mean, we need to tell the truth and plant the seeds.. but we can't make seeds grow. We must drop back and leave the seeds hidden.

33

Homemade Aprons over Bare Feet

Dear Kitchen Saints, Soon .. very soon.. I hope I can get Jim to take me to the Salvation Army. I want to get some prairie skirts to make a few more aprons. They are fun to make. Just pick out a flowered skirt .. soft and cotton.. Then you take your sewing scissors and cut the back of the skirt out.. so that all you have is the front part of the skirt. Then just buy some cotton washable ribbon and sew them to each side of the waistband and you have a nice long apron. Sometimes, if you cut it just right along the side seams then you don't even have to hem the sides. I love the really long aprons to cover my skirts. I may even find some more long cotton skirts for spring... In the warm days I think cotton skirts are so much cooler, even than shorts. Of course I run barefoot all year outside as I hang the clothes on the line and putter in my garden. I promised myself that when I became 40 that I would begin to wear shoes .. As it ain't even decent, a woman my age . a grown mother of 6 children. BAREFOOT.. But I turned 40 and I still don't wear shoes.. and then 50 and now 53. I don't imagine I will ever wear shoes. .well except when I go to town, ya know? When I first started writing, and to my surprise I got published. I would say to the Lord, "But Lord, I don't even wear shoes." I told Christian Joy, my 27 year old, how I felt. She said, "Oh Mom, don't worry about it .. Anyone who reads your writing would already know that you don't wear shoes." So I guess I'm not fooling anyone. .even though I hide behind this email machine.

Well I need to get busy.. just wanted to tell you about the aprons so that maybe you can get some made before spring. I think, for supper, I will fix Papa shepherd's pie. I just put a layer of cooked and drained hamburger at the bottom of a pan. Then put some green beans on the top. Then pour gravy or diluted mushroom soup on top of that. Then I make mashed potatoes and put them on the top and bake them until they are brown. Papa will be needing some gravy by today. He has some errands to run after work so I will have plenty of time to do my gardening plans on paper this afternoon. Well I had better start rattling pots and pans, as Mary Lehman always says when she is starting to fix a meal. Have a good day.

34

Keepers at Home

Dear Keepers, You know what? My writing lately has been different.. The Holy Spirit really has a message in my heart... I really got to thinking, "What is the Lord saying?" I really feel that there is coming like a judgment in the house of God. And He wants we mothers to get our homes in order. So far we have done OK as we have leaned toward the gods of this world. . . Judgment hasn't hit some of us on that one. But for some others of us, our eyes have been opened.. This whole issue is very simple.. God's Word is the only authority. He is our healer, our counselor, our Doctor, our supplier. He is our teacher, our Pastor.. His word is true and His holy order for the family is a better order than what we can dream up on our own. And it is not by might and not by power but by His Spirit that our families will remain intact. I think the time has come that the Lord is saying, to quit trying to make a home with your own ideas ..follow the Master's plan. I am not speaking to the wives who want to work outside the home.. This writing is to the wives who God has called home.

I really feel there is coming an even greater attack on the

family and the mothers at home will play such an important role. It's like if these wives will simply drop back into this place of holy humility.. you will find life so simple and easy.. It's like this humility will take you into another spiritual realm... Submit to your husband as unto the Lord. One of these days folks will say, "Well how did that family even make it . . That wife stays home and doesn't even work while the 2 income families are falling apart.. how does that work?" It's simple, because we are in a spiritual war with Satan and this world's ideas are failing and now we had better see if God's ways will work.. Now that I saw my Dad die in a hospital and saw with my own eyes some things.. I mean I will die at home thanks. And how long will it be before the power-outages hit our area .. it may have hit your area by now. And as you know it doesn't matter how much money you have -- your lights are going off as fast as the poor people's lights. We are in a spiritual war and not a physical war. Money won't make a spiritual war any easier....

Mothers who are called home, be sure to obey the Lord.. Take on His yoke, for His burden is easy...His burden is that of a housewife, for a mother in her home. It's easy to walk in obedience to the Lord.. It's hard.. very hard, to do our own thing.. I don't get the CNN news. .We don't have cable... But I talked to a friend this afternoon who does.. She was saying the news was talking about how will we go back to the time before electricity when we have a lot of power outages? Well it's simple. .just go back.. Get out your kerosene lamps and have at

it. Some folks, when their lights go out, will hoop and holler...
But the saintly mother, called and set a part unto God, will
remain calm.. because she has discerned the times and the
seasons. She is prepared to do whatever it takes to keep her
family safe and full of faith. She is a visionary and has the
imagination of a child.. and God will speak to her in so many
ways as to how to make it without electricity or whatever she
lacks. And she will leap to her feet when she hears Him call..
For her ears are tuned to the Master's voice ...

35

Good Forgivers

Dear Ladies, This afternoon I am baking dinner rolls and cinnamon rolls. Also I made Beef stew with homemade noodles in it. My Jim will be home in awhile from work. It's the afternoon and it is snowing outside. I have felt so close to my husband lately. My heart calls to him even now. As I look out my snowy window, as I write... my memories drop back to when we were in our first years of a very stormy marriage. We would have a fight and Jim would hitch-hike out of town and be gone for a month or so. I would weep my heart out. For days on end. People would say, "Well he is demon possessed ".. and I would agree... Had to agree... and yet I knew I had the answers for Jim ... the Lord Jesus Christ. I used to wonder why no one could understand that, He who was greater in me, was greater than he who was in the world. Why didn't the believers around me understand? I know they hated to see me and the children suffer so. And yet we were in the hallow of GOD'S hands. Jim would then call me in a month or so, long distance from another state. Asking how we were and telling me he was hopeless. That we should divorce and that I needed to just give up and find someone who could be a decent husband. I would say, "Honey.. Come home..." So he would stand out on the highway with his thumb out... in the summer heat ...trying to catch a ride from one state to the next... trying to make his way back home. It would take him days. And I would prepare my heart to greet him. He needed me to help him and to care for him. Now this is not a popular story... especially in this day of easy divorce. ... But yes, Jim needed me .. He needed me to show him the Savior....He didn't know the Lord that I knew. He does now .. but he didn't then. Oh when I would see him coming up the street, sun parched face and ragged clothes.. my heart would leap.. how I had missed him... How I loved him with an everlasting love. I gave up many times and was bitter ...very bitter. But then I would forgive him and it would be alright for a while.

We were talking about this .. this morning with Mary. I said, "Mary... Papa really needed me.. when we first married." Well he still does and I need him so much. As a Christian wife I am so happy that the Lord called me to a man who really needed me. Of course, now Jim has been saved for over 20 years. And, as I was telling a friend, Jim spoils the kids and I rotten. He isn't a rich man but he certainly spoils us with Love. Many times, over the past 20 years, he has had to forgive me too.. I needed his strength and forgiveness as he had needed mine. I tell people that Jim and I don't have a good marriage because we are so easy to get along with. We are just two "good forgivers." No one is perfect.. we are all flesh and blood. We are all going to need forgiveness from our mates at one time or the other. When you are called upon to forgive your man... Forgive him as you would want to be forgiven... Because your day will come and you will need your husband to have a patient and forgiving heart. What you put into your marriage, you will receive out of it...

36

Housewifery

Dear Housewives, I am so happy this morning. I got a good sleep last night...Today I get to do some deliberate homemaking. Many of my days are days of playing catch up. The meals are hurried and it's run here and there to pick up because we need to do this or that. Unexpected company comes... I run to clear the table and to get out my teapot and china cups. Making a not -very- nice tea party for a friend. A best friend came yesterday unexpected. I was so tired from the activities of the days before. .I was embarrassed of the house right after my friend left to go home .. Jim came home from work and we had to go to the store.. When we got back home I was playing catch up again with supper. And having said all of that... I am happy to say that today will be a good day of intentional housekeeping. A day to make soup.. to take my time and putter about the house doing things that take some thought. I have my groceries bought and Mary always vacuums and does the straightening up anyway, each day.... She does a lot of the wash too. But I have a lot of little piles of odds and ends that need to be put away by mother only.

I am especially anxious to get into my kitchen and make little displays while I am making potato soup. I have an old Hoosier cabinet in there. I love to take everything off the working space and put an old fashioned tablecloth on there... before I get to cooking. I love to imagine what the mothers in the 1800's did to make their homes look cozy and pretty; Especially in the wintertime. I am sure they stayed in their kitchen and baked a lot, to just stay warm. And especially in the cold mornings. So I will turn my oven on too and start something baking, before I do my cleaning or make soup. As I do my dishes, I will imagine that behind me is a real wood stove ... a big old fashioned HOME COMFORT wood burner. I will imagine an old gray barn as I look out my snowy window. As I take my old potato peelings out to the garden, I will imagine that I am feeding the chickens out by the hen house.

My dollies ...Mary's and Christian Joy's dolls really... are thrown in the corner. They are still in their spring outfits. Today I will put their winter clothes on them and fix the living room up. I have even been too busy to light my kerosene burner in there. I am so home sick to really be home....not just in body .. but in my spirit. I hear the proverbs voice of wisdom call me to work with my hands. She calls me to my heart's desire. I call wisdom my sister and understanding my kinswoman. They stand here with me as I write.. Telling me, "The wise woman builds up her home and the foolish woman tears it down with her own hands." A precious cloud of witnesses stand with me and whisper courage to me and faith.

Sarah is here and Elizabeth... my favorites; and I sense Mary and Hannah. Each giving me teachings on faith and courage. I welcome them and the angels.

Last night I prayed most of the night. The few hours of sleep I did have was life giving and worth 14 hours of sleep with burdens in my heart... My burdens are gone this morning and I feel happy. I really need to go... but first I wanted to share my recipe for potato soup. I just make it like you do probably. I just cut up potatoes and put them in a big pot to boil. When they are about half done. .I mash them in chunks. Then I add onions and some carrots.. and celery. . and finish the cooking.. Then I add milk at the end.

37

An Old Time Marriage (Part 1)

Dear Mothers , It's 7:00 AM. . Jim just went to the store for some things and I will have a little time to write. .I have felt so serious lately . . I dunno exactly why. .This morning, I woke up anxious. I often think of the injustice that goes on around me and it breaks my heart. .My friend Rose called last evening. .She was telling me about her lil' granddaughter and how a Dr. mistreated her, It is so sad. .This morning, as I read my Bible and prayed I asked the Lord about so many that are hurting. . And the question always comes up, "Why do bad things seem to happen to good people, while the sinners get by with murder?" And the Lord spoke to my heart and told me that I had been hurting for many years but He was there to deliver me. .And ya know, I don't know why I was delivered out of the lion's den, but I was. .And now my life is very peaceful. .Oh I joke about Jim poppin' someone in the nose. .But ya know, that was many years ago. .I have to tell you that Jim never gets behind in his bills. .He has worked for many years now ..I don't worry like I used to. . Jim has made a peaceful place for me to live now. .My children aren't perfect ..But I have a quiet home to pray for them. .My life is quiet enough to be able to fight spiritual battles and win them. .Jim wouldn't ask me to go to work.. Nancy was here last week and when she left she said something- what she often says.. "Connie, I am so glad you are alright now. .both you and Jim." She was able to see that my home was at peace and rest.. I have seen both sides of married life ..I was certainly taken through a horrid nightmare for many years. .But the Lord did reward me for my faith. .I do see women around me who were faithful too and were never delivered ..and this breaks my heart. .Nevertheless, my testimony is that I was sinking in the miry clay and the Lord set me upon the rock to stay. .My testimony is that God said and did what he said He would do. .In my despair the Lord said to me. ."Connie, call upon me and I will answer you and show you great and mighty things that you know not." And He did do that ..He has shown me His power and greatness that I could never imagine. .He has given me exceedingly and abundantly more than I could ever think or ask.

I remember when I only had 3 children. .I constantly prayed for more children. .And Jim told me we wouldn't have any more ..Later on, after he was healed, he asked me to have more children and we had 3 more. .The Lord has been so good to me. Yes we have been poor. .But ya know, when you go through what I did, being poor isn't anything to you. .Last evening as I watered my garden I thanked the Lord for a garden hose to water with. .And I thank the Lord that I don't ever worry about the water bill or any of the utilities . .All of this worry used to be mine. .Now when Jim asks me to not use a lot of water, I understand how he feels. But I take no care or worry over any of our bills. .All of this is upon my husband.

Last evening, Jim made pretty good with his tips. .I had to use some birthday money I had put back to buy groceries this week. .As soon as Papa made some money at work, he brought it home and told me he would repay me for the money I used of my birthday money. .Of course I said, "No Honey. .just wait until you are back on your feet and then pay me back if you want to." I thought it was so precious of Jim not to want me to use my money for groceries. .And for him to barely get any money and want to give it to me.. But that is how Jim is. .His heart is always to me and what he thinks I may want. .He can't barely stand it if he thinks he has hurt my feelings in any way. . And I am the same with him. .Rarely do Jim and I fight over anything. .And if we do, we both take the blame from each other. ."It was my fault." He will tell me, and I will argue it was my fault. .Or he will want me to have something extra and I will say, "No you take it." A marriage like that comes out of many trials...

38

An Old Time Family (Part 2)

And oh am I feelin' old lately. Over the 4th, we had John and his wife and our grandson, Romeo, for a week. .Oh they are a riot and so much fun to have. .I also took care of Baby Rose ..I am still trying to rest up. My kids all LOVE firecrackers and they are illegal in Iowa. .John brought hundreds of dollars worth of crackers to our house ..Of course the police came. . John shot off "some" firecrackers that were supposed to be for children. .But they went clear over the house. .He said, "Mom, I have never seen that fire cracker do that before. .It usually just spins around.". .I knew it was because I was standin' there.. And I am so full of fire and he is too and God knows anything could happen. .John shot things off that went over my head and the debris fell on top of my head and anyone else's head who was nearby .It's a wonder I am still alive. .So anyway, forgive me if I ain't up to snuff lately. .You wouldn't be either if you were me. .But things are quiet now. .And each day I get up in the morning and tell the Lord that I am so glad all that is OVER!!..If John could have tied me to a firecracker and shot me over the moon, he would have. .Come to think of it, I would have been game for it if ya wanna know the truth. . But I would have paid for it in the morning. .I am tired and I ain't springin' back like I used to. .I guess I am beginning to realize that I am getting old. .Papa keeps tryin' to tell me that. But its kinda hard to fall into it ..Jim just got back from the store and I told him I was writing about the 4th ..I reminded him of that firecracker of John's that was supposed to just spin? It went across the street and over the neighbor's house. Our poor neighbors!!! Jim was laughin' with me over John and his firecrackers.

John is our 3rd child. .the one who ran away and I hardly saw him for 7 years. Oh what a heart he has for Jim and me now. . . Johnny has so much love.. When he was young, he loved to play with fire.. He used to get up on the balcony of our house and make paper airplanes and light them on fire. I would be downstairs and wonder why all the black paper was drifting down the windows. .it was burnt paper. .And often I would see folks gathering outside our house and looking up. .I knew my boys were doing tricks on the roof. .One neighbor family told me that they gave up watching TV in the evening; they just sat outside in the summer and watched our house. . As the mother of the circus performers, I was none too happy with my children. .Jim was always yelling, "And this is why I have holes in my roof!" And I was always trying to yell at John through a whisper as not to rile Jim up.. "Johnny, you are goin' to burn our house down. .and we don't have any insurance." And low and behold, John never did burn the house down, but I nearly did twice ..

My dear sister- in- law, Kriss, bought us a fire alarm for

upstairs. .The boys took it apart and used the parts for other things ..And gosh we sure could have used that fire alarm. . When Jimmy was in the Navy he would bring home bombs to give away to the boys for Christmas presents. They were bottle rockets that went off under water. .So the boys set them off under the snow.. "Merry Christmas and Happy New Year"!!!!! So actually, I am a 58 year old mother in the body of an 80 year old woman."

When Jimmy was 12, our first son, he kept beggin' me for gun- powder. . Jim was just saved .. Anyway, I kept telling Jimmy, "No, of course not. ." Well, finally I got so put out with Jimmy, I told him to go ask Jim. .I figured Jim would threaten Jimmy and tell him off and that would be the end of it. .But no, Jim says, "only a pound" ..Boy did Jimmy have a good summer. No one will ever forget it. He made bombs in the root cellar all summer. .When guests came to the house to visit and the explosions were going off, I acted like it was nothing. . Jimmy bought 2 by 4's and drilled the inside out and packed them with gun powder....WHAT A SUMMER THAT WAS!!!

39

Faith And Nest Building

Dear ladies, Last evening I got an email from a wife representing a very hurting family. I told her that my writing today would be pointed at her. Some of we wives have started out our married lives building our nests in a tornado. But we got it built and then a fire burned it down. We have begun again and again and again. Just for the record, my nest fell apart over 30 times in the first 12 years of my marriage. People walked by ..shook their heads and said, "Well there is no hope for that nest. That's for sure." I would pray and tell the Lord I was finished... "I am not going to try to stick this nest back together again." I'd pray, "I'm tired Lord ..can't you hear me? I'm tired.. Let me out of this disaster." For awhile, I would roll over and play dead. You know, stay in bed and not get up for days....not eat. . pray to die. etc. Well need I say more? I KNOW where some of you are at. But you know ladies... dog - gone it .. you can win this fight if ya want to? I found out the devil wasn't all that big. And if you give the Lord TIME he will make "OLD SLY" hand you a grand testimony. Now don't tell me He won't. . and don't try to match war stories with me.. cause I will win.. I always win when matching war stories. It's your vision ladies.. what is in your heart? If it's defeat, then that is where you will go. "My people perish for lack of vision" . . . . Think of Thomas Edison who discovered the light bulb, or any of the great inventors in our country. It was trial and error again and again and again. They just never gave up. Look at Sarah.. she just refused to give up. Oh mercy can you imagine being barren all of your life until you are OLD, then the Lord tells you that you will have a baby and his descendents will be as the sand? I mean Sarah must have given up a million times throughout her lifetime, thinking she would never ever get pregnant. But she didn't give up. . she was a woman of virtue. Ladies of suffering, you must get alone with God and cast down vain imaginations and give Christ your imaginations. And let Him create an image ...His imaginations in your mind. Let Him be creative with you and think big... Don't limit God. Submit to His word.. Don't be lazy and say, "Well whatever will be will be." Work at it Ladies.. and fight the good fight of faith. You only have one life to live for Christ. Those children you have are only under your care for such a brief time. As you learn faith .. teach it to your babies. . .as you go. Ask and you will receive that your joy will be full. Let your children's joy be full too. God isn't going to let you all down. At least twice my children have gotten a report from the hospital that, "your mother may die." My kids always said, "Mom we knew you weren't gonna die". . .It takes a lot to scare my kids.. They think our family can do anything. I just never tell them we can't. I never told our kids we were poor.

They never found out until they got out among people. We never went to doctors except for emergencies. Well sometimes not even then. Jimmy, our oldest son, said he doesn't even remember going through hard times. Most of it he laughs about. It was so horrid, at times, we all had to laugh about it. It would get so bizarre .. Man, I HAD to laugh. I always knew the Lord would have me write about it someday. I always thought if God takes me out of this, the world is gonna hear about it. When I ask Jim if I could go to 90 countries with our story. He thought I was kidding..

40

Old time Families (Part 1)

Dear Mothers, I am up extra early this morning. .It's about 4:30. .Thought I would write down some things I have been thinking of about the role of the wife and mother. .Ya know, back in the old days, families stayed together. no matter what. Once ya got married, then that was it. .The icing on the cake was that you had a happy marriage. .But no one divorced if they didn't have happiness or fulfillment in the marriage. . Folks would say, "Well we stayed together under difficult situations because of the children. .We didn't want to mess up their lives or make 'em choose between us." And many a couple lived in a hard situation but bore it to give the children a home. .When I was a young girl growing up in the 1950's, I barely knew of a divorced person. . The neighbor women around me were stay- at- home mothers. .Some of the families were happy and some were not. And then as the mother and dad put the children first instead of each other, they did have many happy times as a family. .They kinda grew together and learned to somehow put up with each other . . And somehow all of these families made up a more gentle society. .and a more sane Nation. .

The Mother of the home was a rock for the most part. I

remember only a few days, as a child, that supper wasn't ready at 5:00 in the evening. My Grandfather, who was living with us, had died and Mom found him and she got so upset she had a miscarriage. So when my brother and I got home from school, my Dad was there to fix supper for us. I remember being scared as Mom was always there and now she wasn't ..I will never forget Dad as he had just lost his Father. .My Dad thought it was sissyish to cry ..So he hid his tears from my brother and I as he hid behind the cupboard door. He pretended to look for something to feed us for supper. .Dad was in his 30's ..I will never forget the sight of him that lonely evening as he tried to fix supper for Scott and me. He wiped his eyes as the tears dropped from his face. .

Dad had been an orphan and this wonderful man whom he called, "Dad," rescued him. .Grandpa's name was Frank and he and his wife couldn't have children ..This was during the Depression era. .And Frank was to minister to many of the poor children in the neighborhood. . They called the place where they lived, "the bottoms"- or the poor section of town...Often Frank would give food away or help with coal to give to needy families for their stove in the winter. .He took in many children and gave them temporary homes or adopted them. .My Dad's Mother was also adopted by Frank. .Her name was Jaunita and later in her life she got saved and married a man who became a preacher ..He preached in an old shack to the poor people in the bottoms. .One stormy windy night, Granddad was preachin' a mighty sermon and the glory fell and the shack almost fell down because of the storm. .The deacons went out and took poles and held the shack up until the preachin' was over and souls were saved. .Jaunita {my grandmother} played the piano and the accordion. .I didn't know that Jaunita was my grandmother..She came around with her husband to our house ..I thought they were just family friends, because I had only known my adoptive grandparents. .But Jaunita had gotten saved in her 40's and she wanted to make it right with her son ..my Dad.. So she started to come around to our house to visit. .Finally, my folks told me and Scott that Jaunita was our real grandmother. Of course she then tried to tell my folks about the Lord and how He saved her. .Well they didn't want any part of it ..They told Jaunita to never tell me about the Lord ..But Jaunita prayed ..but never really spoke to me about the saving knowledge of Christ. .At Christmas they invited our family to church and we went out of tradition. .Oh that old church was so full of Holy Ghost Joy. And Jaunita and her husband gave all the poor folks presents. .And sacks and sacks of Christmas candy was given to the poor children. .

41

Old time Families (Part 2)

Ya know, back then if parents told a relative not to say certain things to their children, then they didn't. So Jaunita just prayed for our family to come to Christ. Finally when I was 19 I received the Lord. And while I was a child, Jaunita crafted many dolls for me for Christmas. Jaunita had the dark hair and brown eyes. But each Christmas doll had the dark hair and blue eyes like mine. Later when Grandmother Jaunita died, I was in her bedroom. A small picture of me was on her dresser mirror. On the back of the picture it said, "My Baby" ..Secretly she had prayed for me for many years to know the Lord. She never had any more children, only my Dad. .and she so longed for children...I was to have 6 children. .I know because of her prayers...She visited my family home with Jim just a handful of times. .The last visit she had here before she died was so unforgettable. I was apologizing for the messes the kids made. .And Grandma said, "Oh Connie you had all the babies I never had. .just be thankful that you had them." ..After Jaunita died, my mom cleaned her house out and then gave me a big sack of Jaunita's old bath towels. .One evening as I had bathed my little ones, I got out the towels that were Jaunita's. .And the children wrapped up in the towels as they laughed and played in the house. .I could feel Jaunita in heaven so full of joy sensing her many grandchildren wrapped joyfully in her bath towels. .

Many years later, just before my Dad died, he received the Lord. .He had broken his pelvis and yet got out of bed and kneeled finally before the Lord ...Dad had dementia in his old age. .I would sit with him and sing to him about Jesus. .Often he couldn't talk to me. .But just a few days before he died he made it right with God. .Mom came in the bedroom to find him on his knees praying...he died about a week later. .

So through it all, Jaunita's prayers were answered. And now I have had the blessing of winning some souls to Christ. .But we ought always to pray as mothers and wives, and never give up. .We don't know who will be saved ..We are just called as keepers at home to be faithful. .To show a pattern of good works. .Our marriages may not be sunshine and roses all the time. .Most long- time married folks have many heartaches in their families. .it's a rare family that doesn't have a few scars. .

. .But Mother has to remain as a bulwark and stalwart of faith. . .She must remain when everyone else has given up. .Her faith must stay strong as a mountain. .Because some day her time on earth will be over and her work done. .The things she neglected to do or say will never be said. .She is the children's mother and no one else can take her place. .As she loves her husband and comforts him she does the work of the Lord. .

Leave the making of the man's soul for Christ, with Jesus. .As wife, just comfort him and love him. .Pray and give your family to Jesus and let Jesus take the burdens. .Dear Mothers just make a home and decide today to never give up. .Stand strong and full of courage as the Lord is on your side.

42

Country Mothers (Part 1)

Dear Mothers, I am up and about getting ready for the day with Baby Rose. Yesterday we were to have her, but David didn't have to work so I didn't have her after all. Jim and I went to the Garden Shop and I found some Feverfew. .That is an herb and if you have a headache it is supposed to help you. . You are supposed to chew the leaves.. When I had it before, I chewed the leaves in with some Spearmint gum ..It is a perennial and looks like daisies. .I hope to get a good patch of it goin' in my herb garden ..I also got some more Lavender. It was almost 90 here in Iowa yesterday. .I didn't get anything done in the garden, it was just too hot. .But it has to get real hot for tomatoes to grow. .So the tomatoes were happy but no one else was. .

All yesterday morning I was thinkin' about the old time housewives. .And yesterday in the afternoon I was doing some reading. I have this old pioneer book. .It has poems and stories. .One was written by a pioneer woman. And it was about how she needed so many things to run her homestead. . But what she prayed for the most each day was courage. .Oh God Bless America. .don't we need courage as Mothers for this day and age? This society is so corrupt ..It just makes ya wanna roll over and play dead. Hu? But I think this is how it has been in many troubled times in the past too. .Of course the Depression era was filled with hard times. .I think like now, somewhat. .But ya know if we have homes and a roof over our heads and kitchens to cook in and beds for our children, then we should praise the Lord. Ya know, in the old days the farm mothers got up around 4 in the morning to start their work. . And ya know, they didn't even have fans for this hot weather. But they cooked and baked bread, cakes, and pies nearly every day. .They did their cooking in the cool of the day. .Often they had a make shift shed out back that they made into a summer kitchen. .This way the wood stove didn't heat up the main house. .They had a big noon meal usually and got their cooking out of the way as the day got hotter. .Then for supper, they had the leftovers from the noon meal. .Many of the men were farmers and home for lunch. But the old time mother did most of their summer work in the mornings. .Then in the afternoon they rested and the children napped. .

When I would go to my aunt's farm to stay a few weeks in the summer, this is how the farm women did it. .My Gram lived in a little house in the back yard of my aunt's house. .And Gram would help with the garden, or the cooking, or whatever. .But the hot summer afternoons were quiet as the Mothers rested. . I think it is important to work hard but to rest too. .We need time as mothers to be refreshed ..To talk to God and to regroup as the children nap. .Then after naps, it is time to prepare the house for the evening meal. The rest of the day is sorta to prepare to wind down for the evening. It's a time for work, but a time to get ready for the evening. So you fix supper and then later it's time to make sure the children have their baths and get their rooms ready for them to go to bed. .Get the dishes done and the supper food put in the ice box. .It's time to read a story to the children and a time for prayers. .After the children are in bed, Mother may want to have another time to read the word and pray. .But Mother goes to bed pretty early herself as she has another big day to tend to the next morning. . . I remember when I was raised in the 50's. .My brother and I thought my mother never slept. .if we were to go in her bedroom at night she would be laying there with eyes shut. . And she would hear us and say, "Don't step on my glasses." Mom always kept her glasses right on the floor next to her bed so she could find them in an instant if us kids needed something in the night..

43

Country Mothers (Part 2)

When my Mom and Dad and we children would go to my uncle's farm in the summer, we thought my aunt Jean never slept. .All of the cousins at night slept on the living room floor on quilts. .Late in the night. . I would wake up and see a light in aunt Jean's kitchen.. I would hear my aunt Jean making cold sandwiches for the next day. The old time Mothers never seemed to sleep.. They were up in the night and always up early the next morning. .Of course they rested in the afternoon and this was their salvation.. These Mothers were like firemen. They were always ready to care for the children, even in the middle of the night..

44

Plant lil' Grocery Stores

And ya know, I don't have the perfect garden. ."Land sakes No". .and the siding on our house is doin' some serious falling off. .And the roof leaks, STILL, like a sieve when it rains. .We have had the hole in the kitchen ceiling fixed at least 20 times...It will be fixed for a few years and then it leaks again...And the foundation of our house is awful too. .But the Lord tells me, "Connie you just make your garden and take care of Rose and don't worry about it. .Jim will take care of it." And ya know, this is how it used to be in the old days. .Many times a man would buy a piece of land he felt he could work to feed his family on. .The family would live off the land. Then they wanted to have a cash crop too.. But the husband never looked at the house. . He just looked at the land. .The wife and Mother was to make a home out of whatever house she got. . And Mama would get busy in the spring and plant tiger lilies around the foundation of the house to hide the crumbling foundation ..She would scurry about in the spring and plant all kinds of flower gardens to make bouquets for the family table . In the winter, she dried flowers upside down to give color to her lil' winter home. .Then she was expected to plant things that come up each year ..She called Rhubarb plants ..pie plants .. She would trade seeds with the other country mothers. It was her job to plant the herb garden. .As one mother was thinning out her raspberry plants, she would give the other country mothers some raspberry starts. .Ya know, Mother was expected to make a house a home . . To take control of her home and land and make it work .Usually the husband was too busy making a living to worry about the house fallin' in on one side. .

My friend Jill and her husband moved into an old farm house about 10 yrs ago. The back side of the house was sinking so bad they couldn't close the back kitchen door. .So they hoisted it up with rocks and then the back door closed. .The old time Mothers just made a home out of whatever they had to work with. The home wasn't made perfectly for them? They had to make it. .And the Mothers would plant many perennials . . plants that come up each year. They would plant strawberries and horseradish and rhubarb , and asparagus. . They would start their grape arbor and plant as many fruit trees as they could.. They would also plant walnut trees and other trees that bore nuts. All of these I just mentioned will come up each year. .Then of course they would plant their herb gardens. Herbs for cooking and for medicine...Mother planted ginger root to spice her ginger breads and cakes and to make ginger tea. .She knew the names of all of the flowers and herbs and taught this to her own daughters. Mother would forage in the woods to find wild lettuce, onions and other wild greens in the spring.

See our country used to be a lot different and the land produced many herbs and wild foods. .Now with the poisons put on our land to kill weeds...many of the wild herbs are dead.. And it is not good to use this stuff as it kills many of the health giving herbs and wild foods like the little wild strawberries and other wild berry plants. .Then the poisons sink into the ground and hurt your water supply. We need to say, "the Hell with the perfect yard," and plant little grocery stores in our yards. .Yes the mint will spread and take over the yard. .well so what? Who wants grass? I would rather have a yard full of mint to mow. .Think of how good it would smell to mow mint instead of grass. .Mint and other herbs popping up in the grass is a good thing. .It is medicine growing in your yards ..don't kill it.

During the 1930's, many families lost their homes and were forced to live in the country in abandoned farm homes. .Had the Mothers not known how to make a home out of nothing, the families would not have survived. In our present generation we mothers need to learn to work and prepare while the sun shines...

45

Making Hay While the Sun Shines

This spring, Papa planted a cherry bush called "Sugar Cherry." Also a dwarf peach tree. .We have several dwarf apple trees and a plum tree. .All of these plants come up each year. . Then plants, like tomatoes and peppers, and other garden vegetables just last for the season. .You have to plant them each year. .But ya know, dear Mothers, the old saying is, "Make hay while the sun shines." In other words, you can't bale hay to store for the winter when it's raining. Wet hay will rot and won't store well. And we need to seriously consider our ways in these troubled times...Things are hard now, but Darlin' they are gonna get harder yet. .We need to put some of our money into buying fruit trees and food plants that will come up each year. .Many of you know nothing about the herbs or how to use them. .Now is the time to go to the library and get books and store up knowledge ..Go to book sales and buy books to have at home for a Mother's Home Library. . Books on gardening and herbs and home remedies. .So many people are afraid of herbs, but not of the harmful drugs from the Dr...The medical profession is in serious trouble. . It's time to break loose from them and find your own ways through the wisdom of God. .If you need a certain herb, then learn to grow it and use it ..if it is possible. Gather canning jars this summer while the Garage Sales are plentiful ..Buy some big pans with lids to do some serious home canning this fall. Gather wisdom and confidence that you can make it. .That if push comes to shove, that you could make your own soap for laundry and baths. .The more knowledge you can store up, and the more you can learn now the better. .If you have wisdom and know-how, then you don't need to be afraid of the coming hard times. .Dear hearts, build your confidence now.. Learn the many survival skills of housewifery. .Come back to the land now and learn all you can.

My yard isn't huge, but is big enough to have 2 gardens and 4 dwarf fruit trees. .and many perennials. .If you are in an apartment, you can store up knowledge through books for when you can move to where you have some land. .You can start some tomato plants or green peppers in the big 5 gallon buckets. .But do something to store up knowledge, for the hard times that will surely come. .Especially the families who plan to have many children. .Of course Papa and me just have Rose now. .But I want to be an example to my older children and their families. .Our son Johnny, age 29, ..married with our first grandson, told me while he was here visiting a few years ago, "Mom your whole yard is a garden." And Mothers I would just encourage you to do what you can this spring and summer to learn what you can.. Maybe you can only work on making a Mother's Home Garden Library. .But just do what you can. .

and give some priority to storing knowledge and survival
skills. .

46

Morning Chores

Dear Mothers, Good Morning ..I got up about 4 A.M. and used up the rest of my potato bread dough I had in the frig. .I had made up so much dough . .About the size of half a bed pillow when it rose. .I don't use a recipe, so sometimes I make a lot. .more than I think I am making. .One thing I made a few days ago is this: I took about 2 cups of the hamburger meat I had fried up, remember? With the green peppers and onions.. So I put into this a drained and rinsed can of sour kraut and a can of Pizza sauce. .Stirred it up and made like a calzone filling ..then I put this in some of the rolled up bread dough. .I let it rise with the mixture in it and then baked it. .It was so delicious. .I made a huge thing of it. .After it was baked, I put butter and Parmesan cheese on the top, while it was hot from the oven. .We shared some with our neighbors and they loved it too. .I still have some of the calzone left and I put it in the freezer. .This morning I finally used up the rest of my potato bread dough. .I made cinnamon rolls. .I made a special Cinnamon Bun for Baby also as she will come to visit today. . For dinner preparations today, I just took a frozen beef roast out of the freezer and put it in a pan with some onion and salt and pepper and some water and will let it bake all morning. . Jim has to work later this afternoon ..so we will have our family meal at noon. In a few hours, I will take this meat out and slice it half done as it will slice better that way. .Then I will put it back in the oven and bake it until it is tender. . .a few more hrs. .a bit more water, and the lid on the top . .It's about a 4 pound roast so this will last us for many meals. .But ya have to slice it all up when it is half done. This way you get the nice even slices ..Otherwise, if the meat gets stringy then you can't slice it..

47

A First Year Homestead (Part 1)

Dear Pioneer Sisters, Here are some ideas to start out with when, or if, you were to move to a cabin in the woods. .This is what I would do if I knew I had to eventually be totally self-sufficient and I had a family to care for.. Ok. .it's spring as it is now. . May 13th.. And say I was to move in about a month. I would begin digging up some of my perennials in my yard here.. and bring them to my cabin to plant ..I would make a small homestead garden there too ..Since it is my first year, I would plant just tomatoes, green peppers, cucumbers, some lettuce, and radishes. . and a good crop of onions...For the first year, I wouldn't plant a lot as I would want to get chickens and a chicken house made for before winter. .Around here it is fairly easy to get potatoes cheap and carrots.. And you can buy fresh corn on the cob practically for a song. .So I wouldn't worry my first spring about plowing up a corn field or a potato field. .Carrots are another fresh vegetable that I can buy cheap. . . Carrots will last practically forever in the frig; and they don't need to be canned or frozen. .Just keep a close eye on them and if one gets rotten, throw it out before it rots them all. .I would buy a few bushels of apples for the first year and store them in a cool place for the winter. .But the first spring, I would plant apple trees and other fruit trees on my land. That first year I wouldn't worry over potatoes and carrots, or corn, as they are easy around here to come by. And would be too much work for that first year.. Also, I wouldn't plant a lot of beans to mess with the first year...I mean enough beans to have for summer meals, and peas too ..But going to the Homestead the first year, I would just buy the dried beans and split peas and lentils etc.. They are easily stored in jars and nothing to worry about. .I mean, if one of the Sisters shares her garden beans, then Praise God and can them up for winter. . . But the first year is gonna be hard and dried beans will get ya through. .And I couldn't live without my herbs and I would be haulin' all of those to my cabin ..

What I am tryin' to say is that first year of planting will be a lot of work without over doing it ..Then as you are established, begin planting more in your garden the next Spring. Then I would get a goat and learn to milk her and care for her in the spring. .Even if the family doesn't drink it straight up, you can cook with it and make cheese and soap maybe next year. .But the main thing is knowledge and learning to care for a goat and milk her . .I wouldn't force the goat milk on my children if they didn't like it. .I would mix it half and half with store bought until they got used to it. .If they are young, they will adapt pretty fast, but older children wouldn't. .Papa ain't gonna drink no goat milk ..I mean maybe in 20 yrs but I ain't gonna hold my breath at that. So in the spring and summer the goat and the chickens will provide a lot of food. .But when the cold weather comes, the chickens won't lay eggs as much. But eggs are easily stored too in the frig. .I have seen directions for storing eggs and it all sounds very complicated to me . .But eggs will last in the frig for months on end. .If an egg is good, you will know it, and if it ain't you will know that too. Just break the eggs open in a bowl before you cook them and you will know if they are good or not. . ..I mean you can get real complicated recipes for storing eggs in lime water or a bucket of lard. . whatever. .But to me, they stay just as fresh in the frig.. I mean providing you have electricity. .And that first year I would for sure have electricity until I got the hang of the other stuff..

48

Homestead Mothers (Part 2)

A few days ago, we were out Garage Sale-ing. .And we came to an area of huge new houses. Two income families with maybe one child.. Then we passed new apt. buildings ..No place for a garden or clothes line. .no place to live or have a dog. .I said, "Oh Papa these poor families are just existing and have so little ..They aren't learning anything.." These poor folks are paying for a lifestyle and not a life. They have run with the herd and bought the lie and will run off the cliff with the rest of the herd. .And its got to be ok, as all of their friends are doing it . How off the wall do you have to be to think our country is doing good and all we need is better schools and education and the right president to put us back on target? I mean, I am no Rocket Scientist ..just a poor housewife really. . But I can tell things ain't goin' all that good in my country.. I don't get this opinion just from watching Fox News which ain't all that good .. But I see folks in dire straits around me. Oh I wish I didn't. .And ya know, Christian Joy has told me that as she sees street kids, she tells them of her Dad and Mom who have made it on practically nothing and they can too...It takes

a pioneer spirit and boy we need to develop this in our souls
..We need to grow some spines of steel and teach ourselves to
just flat out make it one way or the other. .Our nation's homes
were formed from the prayers and the tears of the Pioneer
Mothers who came here with nothing. And if they made it, so
can I. "By golly ..so can I. " And you can too, dear Mothers ..I
need to write more about buying things for your Homestead
Pantry for that first year. .But I will have to get to that maybe
tomorrow. .Duty calls. . .

49

A Homestead Pantry (Part 3)

Dear Mothers ..Good Morning. .Yesterday I was writing about Homesteading and going back to the land. {To understand this writing you will probably need to read the first 2 on Homesteading} One thing I was trying to caution my readers about is not biting off more than they can chew. .I know one time I read an article in *Crowned with Silver* about a dear Mother who nearly died from over work. She had these dreams of moving to a farm with her large homeschooling family. . .Cooking from scratch and having goats and chickens. . . Well she wasn't prepared for any of this and way over did it. . . She and her children got the flu and because of being so stressed, it took a long time for them to all get well again. .Her garden was way too large and she couldn't care for it. .So of course, the city women mocked her and told her that she could never make a go of it on the land. .Well ya know, slow and steady wins the race. .Ya know, if you have a small garden in town and can't keep up with it, then don't try to go to the country and plow up a big garden and add animals to care for to the work. Judge yourselves by what you have done with your small garden in the city.. If you have outgrown your city garden then you are ready to get a bigger garden. .I say all of this to say again, "Make hay while the sun shines." Prepare yourselves now for the coming harder times ahead. .do what you can to learn survival skills ..At different times in my marriage, over the past 40 yrs, I have had to do many things to survive and to keep my family from going under. I was prepared with knowledge and I was glad I was. Ok, now let's say I have my Homestead and I am preparing to move in about a month. Again it is the Spring like now. .I would want to stock my pantry so that I would only have to go to town once a month. .I will be busy with gardening and children and won't have time to leave the Homestead more than once a month. .So this is basically what I would buy. .I would buy a lot of canned vegetables, fruits and meats. .I am shooting for total self- sufficiency but I am not there yet. I will be canning tomatoes out of my garden in the fall. .Until then, I will need some canned items. .So I will buy as many canned items as I can until I learn gradually to replace them all with homemade. . . So I will buy the canned items that I think I could grow in my garden ..Such as canned green beans, peas, and corn, etc.. Ok, Papa's coffee. .a big can!

I am imagining that I have big shelves in my Homestead Pantry. .I would use large glass jars to store macaroni, rice, dried beans, oatmeal, cornmeal, and bread flour. .This way you always know at a glance if you need more beans or whatever. .You just can't beat the big tight lidded glass jars for storage. .

Then of course, you need other baking supplies like shortening, yeast , baking powder and soda for biscuits. .And if ya can't make biscuits, learn now as they come in mighty handy for a big family supper of gravy and biscuits. .Now for me, I use the gravy mixes from Aldies. . We don't eat a lot of meat and so I need these mixes to put in soups, etc. for flavor.. I can make my own soup stock and can it too. .And eventually, if I needed to, I could again. .

I will bring a bottle of ketchup to my homestead but will make many jars of it the coming fall with my homegrown tomatoes. Then of course, you will need big bins in your pantry to store potatoes ..I would also buy a lot of canned milk and instant milk. .I would buy maybe 6 gallons of fresh milk for the month and can some of this to last the month. .I have canned milk before and I know how. .So this is basically it. .Jim is up and I need to go fix breakfast. . .I would have a freezer and an extra frig. my first year of homesteading if I could swing it - Because you will need eggs and meat before you get your flock of chickens established. .But eventually, I would want to can the meat and have a dugout for cold things.

50

Trails of Tears and Joy

Oh back in the old days, Jim and me went to an old time Baptist church. .The preacher would preach and the holy convicting power would fall on the flock of God. .And so many couldn't wait for the sermon to be over so they could run up to the alter and weep over their sins and pray ..Then they would stand back up and turn around with that holy peace in their eyes. And the brothers and sisters in Christ would love on 'em and tell them they understood...being sinners themselves. . And ya know, Papa was a wild cat. .Always leaving us and hitchhiking all over America. .And he would come back home as I loved him, and would pray him home. .And he would stand at the back door as he had been gone for months. .I would greet him and shower him with love. .I would ask him if he was hungry and did he want something to eat? Usually he was hungry as his luck had run out ..and it was time to come back home. .And so I would cook something up for him and I would speak peace to him and water him with my love. .I didn't bring up why did he leave, etc. .I just helped him to get back on his feet. And then I waited on God and His power to fall on my dear husband. .And in about a week, the holy power of conviction would fall on him. He would come to me and look into my eyes and say, with tears falling out of his eyes. "Why do I keep leaving my family? I love you and the children more than I can say." . . . And I would hold my beloved in my arms and our tears would intermingle ..We were so passionately in love and longed so for each other. .I was the praying wife always longing for Jim to change, to do right. . And then we would go to church and the convicting power of the Holy Ghost would fall and Papa would run to the altar and weep and repent again and again, with tears running down his cheeks. . And I would see him as I would open my eyes from praying, and I would go to the front of the church too and slip my arms around him and weep with him, repenting of my own sins in our marriage. .

We were so young and so in love, and longed so to have a real home. .a real Christian home. We loved our children and we wanted stability for them.. And yet Papa was to leave many times and my faith was to remain strong as God was with me, and His strength sustained me. His daily manna fed and watered me as I read the Bible and lived from the fresh food of the bread of life. . At night when I was alone, I slept with the Bible and many study books ..Only Jesus was my life and breath. .and I was to go from glory to glory and to see much heartache and then many victories in Christ. .And we were to go from bad to worse. .And from hopelessness to faith many times. .And then one day after 12 years of separating, and coming back together in repentance, we saw the real miracle come and Jim was to stay home and become the priest of our home..

The plate I had set at the table by faith, and the chair I kept open for Jim was finally filled and I saw a miracle ..My seeds of faith I had planted were growing all along even when I didn't think they were. .Jesus was there all the time in the balcony as He watched His son and daughter in the arena ..He was there all the time making sure the fire didn't destroy us. . He was watching as we were tested and He was wondering, "Can I use them for greater things. .Will they stand and not give up. Can I trust them to see miracles . .Will they glorify me or want the glory for themselves? " He pondered over us and watched us with a Father's heart. .And we learned how to trust in Him and to walk out our miracle and to see many more trials and victories. .And we had lived in a wilderness and our walls had been broken and we were left for dead many times. . And now we are called the repairer of the walls. .How could I ever know that in my sorrow, God was there and planning to use me to teach so many of you who are broken.

51

Stay at Home Mothers

I call myself a big baby when I think of the pioneer mothers. But we, as mothers at home in this age, have a huge burden too. .We are almost an endangered species. .And we fight different things than what the Pioneer Mothers fought.. .if you are still standing after 5 years of marriage, then Darlin' you ain't doin' bad ..But we *present-day* pioneer mothers fight to walk in a spiritual wilderness. .it's much like the physical wilderness the women walked in during the 1800's. But it is still the same, whether we are fighting to walk in a spiritual wilderness or a physical one ..if we don't give up, we will see His glory. .We are mothers who bear fruit. .We bear spiritual and physical fruit. .We have children through our wombs or we adopt children ..We bear spiritual fruit as we win many to Christ and we don't give up. We continue on in God. Satan's big thing is to get us to lay down and quit. .to put the pressure on us continually to give up ..To get us to leave our free "Faith Land" and a place of peace for our children ..He screams at us to give up and go back to where we came from. He screams that our children are not saved and our crops of faithfulness aren't coming up. .And that if we don't stop this dream of staying home, we shall surely starve to death as stay- at- home mothers. .

But faith says to walk on the water…to see things that are not as though they seem. .To walk out our faith ..We can't walk out our faith in the comfort zone. .We must be dealt a hand of cards that says we are out of luck. .and as we fall over the edge and off the page, we cry out to Jesus and He alone is our rescuer. .I have a way of always living on that edge? And I fall over the edge a lot? But we must be eager in God to jump out of the boat and seek to walk on the water…We can either back up, go on back home to Satan's slavery in Egypt ..Or we can go on in God, and face the Red Sea. .But as we step out? The Red Sea will open up for us and give us dry land to walk on. .And we will see miracles in no other way. .

It is faith that moves God and pleases Him. .We cannot get a miracle on our own or in our own strength. .We are not supernatural. .God is the Power and the supernatural. .Many of us need miracles ..and all we need to do is keep on keeping on. .When Satan roars as a lion, we must not fear. .We must not fear what man will do unto us ..We must not believe the evil reports. .The pioneer mothers kept on going in the face of plagues and crop failures ..attacks of wild animals. .The mother who went on in God, saved her family. She didn't eat every bite of Satan's bait and temptations. She knew that it was God's will that she win this victory and she did it all by faith. Now many pioneer women went back to wherever they came from ..back to slavery. .They desired the comforts of home and protection more than the comforts of their God. .

But the victorious Mother refused to believe the lies of the devil and she went on in God. .When she had nothing else to live for, she lived on her faith in God. .Her faith was her meat and drink. .she expected God to send a raven to feed her in the dry and barren land. Common sense said, "Go back ..give up. .quit. .Just lay down and quit. .You have nothing else to live for." ..And yet she had her faith. .She had God and Him alone. .. And as we modern mothers fight spiritual battles, we too must go on in faith.

One woman I read about in the 1800's beat wolves from her door, all day, for days. .Maybe you are like that and the devil continually puts fear in your heart. .Well Darlin' get yourself a faith club, the WORD, and beat those wolves away from your door {your mind}. .Take the word of God and sock it to the devil. .And don't give up. .No matter how many wolves are at your door, just keep sockin' 'em until they are all dead. .I mean why give up in the middle of the fight and let the wolves have your family? I mean, we gotta do whatever it takes..

52

A Faith Journey

Dear Mothers, Last evening I just felt such a quickening in my heart .. the Lord said that He had a surprise for me.. I know that a miracle is about to happen. Jim went out and looked for work yesterday. .but didn't find anything yet.. See we won't get unemployment ..Jim has never gotten it.. So .. I mean, the Lord will have to sustain us.. We have nothing to fall back on.. So this is what makes this such a faith journey.. But I have been here before ..many times, and I am not afraid....I am truthfully not in the least bit afraid.. Now Jim made a small income in the first place. . . Now to go days without an income? Well Papa is better physically.. . much better. The Lord is healing him...Now we didn't have the money to go to the Doctor. .Where would we be had God not healed Jim? But He did, and He always does heal us. .The Lord is faithful. .And when I awoke this morning, I prayed.. I said, "Lord ...I have to tell YOU, I do not desire to pray for money or even a job for Jim.. I desire wisdom above all else that I seek.. I must have wisdom."

Wisdom is the principal thing. And in all thy getting...get wisdom.. Wisdom builds the house. .I weep and fear to lose wisdom more than all the things of this world. .For the fear of God is the beginning of wisdom ..I do not fear this present world or what they will do to me.. I fear God.. Call me a rare bird or a liar...But I do not fear a lack of finances or a lack of anything. .Folks chase money to get money. .But we don't need to do that.. We must chase God - the Father, and he will give us what we need... I do not fear what others fear.. I am not of this world. .I am a spiritual mother .. I fear that I will fail God in the arena of life.. I fear that I will not hear the words when I get to heaven. . ."Well done thou good and faithful servant." My soul burns with desire to understand and know the wisdom of God that builds the house.. Oh the riches will come ..the silver and gold.. I will be a rich woman someday.. I know that. .But oh what is that to me? Physical riches in this present world is trash on the street compared to spiritual riches..

The gold and silver that the Lord speaks of, is spiritual. .You get that first, and then the worldly riches come. .Oh if I set my mind to it, I could pray in some money . .and I may have to before it's all said and done. .And that's the easy part. .The hard part is praying in the true gold and silver. .Ya know, this world is so boring and all its glitter is downright monotonous. . it insults me. .The devil insults me if he tries to get me over in an area of fear concerning finances.. Heck, prayin' money in, ain't hard...Jim used to be a bell man at a hotel.. When I prayed for him, he would make tips galore. .Often he would call me from work to pray if he was having a slow night.. Man I would pray money right out of heaven. .that's easy. Like

someone was saying, you just ask the angels to help you....And
when we need them again in the spot we are in now.. I will do
the same thing. .But I guess I haven't even thought of that yet.

But dear Mothers, please don't limit your riches by praying
for money.. Pray for wisdom ..pray for spiritual silver and gold.
.become a spiritual crafts -woman. .Know the moving of the
Holy Spirit. .know God. .Wisdom is the principal thing.. ..Ya
know what? There has never been a word between Papa and I
about me going out and looking for work? Even though he was
sick. .it never crossed our minds for me to go to work. .And
Why? Because I am worth more here.

53

Seeking Wisdom as Gold

Dear Mothers, This morning as I awoke I prayed "Oh Lord please give me wisdom ..A wise woman builds her house." My place here is to continue to build a home.. My price as I walk in wisdom is far above rubies.. Oh the wisdom of God is so powerful.. it is health to your navel and marrow to your bones . . . I know that you know this.. Prov. 4:7, Wisdom is the principal thing ..Prov. 4:8, Exalt her and she will promote thee. .She will bring thee to honor when thou dost embrace her. .Call Wisdom your sister and understanding your kinswoman. We call wisdom forth, as we do our duties as keepers at home. .We don't get more riches into our homes by going out to work ..because that is disobedience to God and rebellion.. We get more riches into our house as we are obedient to God as keepers at home.. You don't have to run over the top of God's head in order to get riches to feed your family. .Well sure some mothers have to work for a while. .But the Lord will deliver them if they walk in wisdom. .

The lie is, that women who don't work and are stay at home mothers don't make any income.. But there is profit in all labor. .I make a lot of money just staying home praying..

Because as I walk out my place of obedience, the Lord gives me money. .if I need it. .Now to go to a shopping mall is downright hard labor for me...I would pay my mother 20 bucks if she wouldn't ask me to go.. I go with her because she is elderly and needs my company sometimes.. But a shopping mall is a hard place to seek the Lord or to pray silently. .And in my heart I am always needing the Lord.. A shopping mall leaves me bare before my enemies. .Satan shoots darts at me and I have no defense.. I feel like I am alone in an enemy camp. I feel no cushion of the Holy Spirit. And then I have my dear mother saying, "Well what's the matter? Why don't you like to shop here?" And how do I pipe it to her how I feel? My heart burns to know wisdom . . and no wisdom exists at a shopping mall. . Well maybe it is in there some place. Wisdom is everywhere and she cries from the city streets as well as the country roads.. But I can't find her there. .And if I can't find her quickly there, then I feel lost and without my spiritual shield..

I can't wait to get back home to where my canning jars are and my homemaking tools .. My Mary Elizabeth is so full of homemaking too ..She loves the old fashioned homemaking .. I adore my old black iron skillets and Dutch ovens. .Lynetta just recently gave me another Dutch oven with a bale handle. .it's really old. .I think I have used that thing every day since she gave it to me a few weeks ago.. Oh sure, when I was a young wife I wanted NEW this and that all the time ..But through the Lord and chasing wisdom, I learned to put the wisdom of the Lord first, and she has become more to me than material things. Wisdom is my sister.. I call her my sister.. This world is not my kinswoman ..understanding is.. . I cry as I write about wisdom ..she is my example. .We must think on the things of God.. On pie making and rolling pins. On cookie sheets and our ovens. .and cooking tools.. Our gardens and our dresses and aprons.. this is keeping your eyes upon the Lord and His word.. We wives should not be thinking about household finances. .Because it is not our burden to bear. .it is our husband's burden to bear. .And this makes a man out of him so let him have the burden.. Drop it and take up your own burden - that of keeper at home..

54

The Art of B.S. -ing (Part 1)

I think I was born to write this. .That and having Moxie must be my truest calling as a writer. .All day yesterday the devil condemned me and told me that I was a Titus 2 mother on the dark side. .Well I can't help it that my husband is who he is and God had him to lead me. .Jim is a wonderful believer...but not one who would fit well in the local church. I wish Dr. Dobson was my uncle or my cousin. But he ain't. .And I wish I could have twisted Jim around to where he would act like a Baptist deacon. .But I dare say it ain't gonna happen. Not in this life anyway...And if I were you and you are anywhere normal and have a normal Christian family and you like church? Then Lady you are on the wrong channel. .Erase my email and head for the hills and don't look back. .But if hell has a way of finding you when you least expect it, then you came to the right place. .Welcome Home. .Now to the art of B.S.- ing. .It's a part of havin' Moxie. It's biting a bullet with your mouth shut and your eyes closed ..And when someone asks ya how you are .YOU ARE FINE as FROG'S HAIR. .and don't forget it. . Well the word says, "By His stripes I am healed. " So I ain't sick. I ain't in any trouble, as the word says that if I dwell with the Lord, then I am under His wings. .So I don't have any problems.. And if I have one, the word says that anything I ask in Jesus' Name, I shall receive. So all I gotta do is ask the Lord for what I need. He says He will never leave us or forsake us. .So I am counting on that ..trust me. .And a lot of the time I do have this kinda faith. .But not always. .And this is where the art of B.S.- ing comes in handy. .You just act like all is well...give it your best shot. You may be quivering in your boots? But ya just get some Moxie and don't let the devil see ya sweat.. .Ya know, when we had our big fire. .oh man, I was scared. .And after it was over, it started on fire again. .It was one Hell of a way to go. . . let me tell ya...And friends of ours begged me to go with them to their house to stay the night. . Jim had to stay here, as the fire chief told him the house could start on fire again and he should watch it. .I was so upset. .But when our friends asked me to come to their house, I just stood up and said, "Ya know, I am just an old pioneer woman and I will be ok to stay here with Jim." Oh I was dyin' inside.. Scared spitless. .And Chuck, our friend, said "a stick of dynamite wouldn't take Connie out of this house. .No sense in tryin' to talk her into it." And I stayed the night with Jim in our house.

It was so cold ..We had to leave the house several times in the night to go out for coffee as we were so cold ..My nerves were so bad they would well up inside me and I would scream out over and over again in the night. .But Papa was there and he would say, "Connie it is ok. " And I would look into Papa's face by the light of a flash light and I remembered how many nights I cried for him, and about an impossible situation.. And again and again as I looked in Papa's face .. I took courage. . And I thought that if God delivered Jim, then He would help us rebuild our house. The devil had tried to hoodwink me into thinking that my marriage was impossible ..How many times did I practice the art of B.S.- ing when the prison guards said Jim was hopeless. I wasn't gonna let those thugs see me sweat. Ya know, last night I was reading some of my old private writings. . .from maybe 10 yrs. ago...I was practicing Moxie. . . on paper. .I said, "Lord please give me things to say when folks ask me why I use my wringer washer and make my own soap?" Well the truth was, my washer and dryer had gone out and I couldn't afford soap. .But I would tell the neighbors with dignity, "I like to make soap and the wringer takes less water. . and I like to be frugal." Well I was gonna be frugal whether I liked it or not? And that's a way of B.S.- ing ..you act like you like to be poor . .

55

The Art of B.S.-ing (Part 2)

I mean you can get B.S.-ing down to an art form if ya work at it long enough. Jill used to teach it to her kids when they were young and they were on welfare. Tony, who is now a wonderful preacher? He always said He just loved Government cheese. . Well it was good but it was embarrassing going to get it. . Especially if ya didn't have a car. . I had to pull a wagon for about 8 blocks to get it. .and I had so many kids that my wagon was full of cheese and butter. .Jimmy, age 37, who has every educational degree you can imagine, loves to kid me about that cheese. He graduated from Rutgers. .I laugh like crazy and that is all a part of the B.S.- ing. . And Jill and I were so good at it that the church ladies envied us, and when they had a problem they asked us to pray for them. .We had church ladies lined up askin' us to help them. Kinda like Tom Sawyer painting the fence for bein' ornery and makin' it look like so much fun that everyone else wanted to do it.

But I am tellin' ya ladies, sometimes your faith is gonna fail. None of us are perfect and we don't always have all of our ducks in a row. This is when ya gotta pull out your manual on B. S.- ing. .And if ya forget how to B.S. when your faith is gone, then dog- gone- it just go ahead and bull dog your way on through. .Play it by ear and it won't be long until your faith will return and your courage will sustain you. .Jesus Christ on the cross cried out, "Lord why have you forsaken me?" Well God hadn't forsaken Jesus. .The Father was there all the time ..And the Father is watching over us even when we feel that we can't go on and our faith is weak and we feel like failures. .God is with us.. He never leaves us. .And if Jesus the son of God felt forsaken, then we will too. .it just goes with the territory.. But Jesus didn't come down off the cross, even though He was under such pain and duress to think that God had forsaken Him. Jesus was all God and yet part man. He is touched by the feelings of our burdens and sorrows.. But He wants us to be women of dignity and sit up straight and act like women of valor, even though we may be shakin' inside. .He has to be able to trust us in the dark ..When everything is dark and God knows we have done all we know to do right. .And it ain't workin' and we are grieved and feel condemned. But we walk on in the dark with hope in our hearts and the knowledge that we never walk alone. .

I know sorrow and have told the children all was well through many times of brokenness. .I was glad to fix supper in my little kitchen to get away from the family to just cry out all of the nervousness in my heart. Any mother worth her salt has cried and suffered alone. .She refuses to scare the children with bad news or that she has barely enough food to feed them. .I never told my children when I didn't have that much food.. I would tell the older ones at times. .But not the younger ones. .Because if Mama seemed happy, then all with their world was happy. .I bore my burdens often with a joke or a candle light dinner of hot dogs. .We are the MOTHERS. . the major pole that holds up the tent. .We are to seek peace and ensue it. We are to make a home of peace and rest ..We should not be looking at our own needs but at the emotional and physical needs of the family. .We, as mothers, are to die daily and to be the example of courage and righteousness...Our courage is the shield of faith over our families. .We must build our homes upon the rock. .We must be women of strength and dignity no matter how poor or rich we are. .No matter what our husbands do or our kids, who embarrass us to tears. . It will be ok, God is with us. .Read the back of the Book - we win. . . We are more than conquerors. Greater is He who is in us, than he who is in the world...Go on, dear Mothers, by faith. . And when you can't go another step in faith, just B.S. the rest of the way home. .and for cryin' out loud, don't let the devil see ya sweat..

56

Sisters of Joy and Thanksgiving

Yesterday as I was mixing up pumpkin bread I stopped and went in the living room to Papa. .I told him, "Ya know Honey, I enjoy having the older kids come home for the holidays. .but you are mainly my family now. .I want to bless our own home. . .We are not just an extension of our older kids lives. .We have a home and life here too. .We are helping raise Baby Rose and still have purpose in our lives." Papa misses his youngin's and wants them here for suppers at least once a week. But I tell him, "Honey they have their own lives. .they are busy.." The actual Thanksgiving dinner will be at my mom's house. .Of course all of we ladies will bring pies and salads and vegetable casseroles. .My mom is 81 and when I get her age wrong she will say to me, "Now Connie Anne? If you are 58, then add 24 years to that and you have it." Well I come up with 82. .but maybe I am only 57? ..That could be. .But anyway, we girls will do most of the work. But you know, it has always been a tradition for me to have a "Home Thanksgiving" just to bless my own house. . And that is what I will have today for me and

Jim. .Of course Jimmy and Christian Joy will be rollin' in this evening and will get to feel the peace and rest of a Thanksgiving home. .Of course David and Tiff and Baby will come over ..And Dan Elvis and his Suzy Q.. And Mary and Brandon. .I plan to make my pies today to take over to Mom's and some to leave here for the remaining days the kids will be here. .

I made a big pot of stew yesterday for Jim as I had so much other stuff to do. .I always make soup when I bake ..so we can just eat when we are hungry. .But I have a lot left for when the kids come and will make bean soup today . .and have both pots out on the stove.. I have some side pork that I am frying right now. .and my beans are getting ready to boil. .I use all kinds of different beans, split peas and every kind of dried bean I can get. .I just wash the beans in cold water ..Then I put them in a big pot. .I am using my tall spaghetti pot. .I just bring these beans to a boil and shut them off and put a lid on 'em. .Then in about an hour, I'll drain this water off and add new water and add the side pork and onions, celery and other flavorings and let them simmer on the stove all day. .

Another thing I am making today is Cranberry Apple Punch ..In my crock pot I will put in about a half a sack of cranberries and fill the pot half way up with water and then add it the rest of the way with apple cider. .I will add about a cup of brown sugar and cinnamon and whole cloves and a bit of nutmeg. When it is done, I will fish out the cranberries with a slotted spoon. .It's just done after you bring it to a boil and then turn it to low for the day. .it makes the house smell good. .Hey have a good Thanksgiving..

57

Miracles

The Bible says that God is perfecting everything that
concerns us. .And we as Mothers just have to be positive and
kind to everyone. .The law of kindness should be upon our
tongues. .And we should open our mouths with wisdom. Prov.
31:26...We should believe God for everyone around us ..Our
neighbors and anyone who we associate with. .Now I don't
mean let crazy people in the house like I do. .I wouldn't do that
with a houseful of children. .or if I am alone without Jim. . if
my relative comes when Jim is not here, I just tell him that I
am busy. .But I am not going to be snotty about it. .I tell him
the truth, that I am busy and I am...Like if I am caring for
Baby Rose, I won't let anyone in that would interrupt my time
with Baby. .I will get embarrassingly blunt over that. .But our
world as keepers at home becomes peaceful as we pray for
those who we associate with. .And I am famous for looking at
the worst of situations and saying, "Oh that ain't nothin'. .it
will be ok." Well in God all is well. God hasn't fallen off the
throne in heaven. .And I may be shakin' in my boots, but I am
gonna confess all is well. And I get as scared as anyone. .and
sometimes I get more scared than anyone. But if I can say

through trembling lips, "Aw it's ok ..that ain't nothin'." Then I figure I am doin' ok. We fight the good fight of faith. .And our fight is always to enter His rest ..

We have to believe God and do whatever it takes to walk out our faith ..And again I am no Super- Christian, as I feel fear too. .But I think I am maybe a better B.S.-er than some of you. .But my B.S- ing, I think, has become a platform at times for my faith. I mean, I can be as down as a dog. .And someone can call me and ask me if I think their situation is hopeless and I will have a spirit come over me that just wants to tease the devil or make him mad I guess. And I will say, "No, I think your situation is great and you will see a miracle." And when I do say that, my faith begins to rise and the true faith comes forth.. .I just love to make the devil mad and be real calm when everyone around me is goin' nuts. .Well God somehow uses that ..

I guess B.S.- ing is a liftoff to faith...It's like obeying God with your tongue. .It's making your tongue say what God says. .But a small part of my makin' my tongue obey is still "get down, pure Hillbilly B.S.-ing." I won't lie to ya. .I do confess the word. But I have a funny side to me too. .And when I can upset the devil's kingdom with being calm when I am to be crazy? Oh I love it. .and I almost live for those moments.. It's fun and entertaining. .it's like the humorous part of God comes on me ..And it's like an airplane or a rocket stopped in my front yard. .. and a voice says, "Connie, ya wanna go on another Rocket ride?" And I will say to myself. ."Well I am too old for this ..but maybe one last ride. .And I jump on the plane and go with God on another explosion. .But it is very fun to upset the devil's plans; especially when he thinks he has it all wrapped up. .And ya do it by just sayin' in the face of Hell all round ya, "Well Praise the Lord that ain't nothin'." ..And say it as cool as the center seed of a cucumber. I mean ya gotta work on it to say it like that, so that your voice don't quiver under the fear. .Well I had better go as duty calls..

58

Get Down Hillbilly

But I would just keep a few cans of potatoes on hand to use in a pinch. .I would sometimes just cut them each in half and brown them in a pan. .And then just add eggs and scramble them all up together. .Maybe put some cheese on the top after it is all cooked up. .But to have a cupboard with lots of canned goods always made me feel content as I knew I could fix a meal with them. .And I would buy a big 20 pound bag of potatoes about every few weeks . .And if I had plenty of potatoes and hamburger, then I felt like I could do some major cooking.

And ya know, in the old days baloney was a good product. .I remember my grandmother fryin' up the regular round sliced baloney. .She would put a cut in it, half way in, and this way the baloney would lay flat in the skillet.. Otherwise it would bubble up in the center. .So to cut in to the center of the baloney made the meat lay flat in the skillet and brown evenly. . . Or I have cut my sliced baloney into squares and fried it up and added it to the mac. and cheese. Also another thing I would do to make the groceries go farther was, I would buy a big pressed ham and have the butcher shave some for sandwiches ..Then a lot of the ham, I would have him cut it in thicker slabs. .Then I would use a few of these to have fried ham for a nice meal with mashed potatoes and gravy. .But then some of the slabs I would cube up with my knife and I would put this in my freezer in small bags. Then I could put this into cheese potatoes ..or I would make gravy with some. Or I would put the cubes into potato soup. .or in beans. I mean if you have pkgs. of cubed ham in the freezer you can think of a lot of stuff to do with it. .And ya know, a lot of this is just "get down hillbilly" food. .

But it's the contentment that is important when you feed the children. .it's not the vitamins that should take first place in your hearts, dear mothers. .I mean set the table and teach the children to eat at the table and to relax and enjoy their food.. Teach them to pray over what they have and to be thankful for the food that is put before them. .Vitamins are important. But order is more important. .What is the scripture that says that a dinner of herbs served in peace is better than more expensive foods served in strife? I used to about die over the fact that I didn't have orange juice every morning for my children's breakfast. .But the Lord impressed me one day with just giving the children a cut up orange every day. I would just cut the oranges up in fourths ..or you could cut them up in circles. . Little children would just eat probably a half an orange in the morning anyway. .But it is cheaper to give the children fresh fruit than all the juice. .Then throughout the day, have them drink water...And of course I have told you before about the honey milk I would fix for my little ones. .If they were wild and crabby. .I would shut the house down and send everyone home who wasn't my kids. And I would have my little one set up to the table and give them a cup of warm milk with a Tbs. of honey in it. .I would use the instant milk and just warm tap water.. With the honey milk and a homemade cookie or just a cracker this would soothe them. .I would make them lay down and take a nap every day too. .I would put them in bed with some books to read. .Even when they were like a year old, I put them to bed with cloth books. .And when we homeschooled, we always took the afternoon off for a nap and reading for an hour after lunch. .And then at 8:00 at night, I put the kids in their rooms to do free reading and then they had to have the lights out at 9:00. .But I tried to keep a quiet household. .and to have hot meals at scheduled times. .This is what makes our homes Christian homes - is the order. .The opposite of a Christian home is a wild home ..Kids eating sandwiches all over the house and fallin' asleep on the floor? That is gonna make a child wild and hard to reason with. .Children need to be taught order..

59

Kitchen Klatter (Part 1)

Dear Mothers, The other day my neighbor Trudy brought me over a big stack of these little housewife magazines from the early 1970's. .They were a takeoff of a radio program that aired each weekday morning ..The Magazine is called "Kitchen Klatter." Then they sold housewife products in the magazine to support it, I guess. .But they have Kitchen Klatter spices and extracts and dish and laundry soaps advertised. The publication was 20 cents apiece or a dollar a year for a subscription.. In the magazine they had stories told about the old days. .Also many recipes ..poems and stories about their children. How to make your husband happy, etc. .Well one of the stories I just loved was called "A Log Cabin Kitchen". .

The grand daughter was writing about her own grandmother. . Grandmother's name was Anney Lee. Anney had 9 children and lived in a little cabin back in the 1930's. . Her husband built her a new house but he left the log cabin in the back of the house so that Anney could do her weaving of rugs that she often sold to buy things for the home. .Her new home had a nice big kitchen to work in and her husband was proud of the home he had built for his Anney Lee. .But Anney was so used to her log cabin fire place and her old stove in the cabin. .She loved it in the winter as her fireplace made the whole cabin so warm and cozy. .Also she had all of the big cooking pots that had been her Mother's and Grandmother's that she cooked with over the open fire. .In the spring and summer, the cabin was so cool and she loved to sit in her wooden rocking chair in the evening and sew and enjoy her cabin. .Finally since Anney didn't use her new kitchen, the family made a bedroom out of it for some of the children....She tried to spend some time in her new kitchen as the children grew up and left home. .But when the grown children gathered back home for the holidays and the grandchildren were growin' up, Anney Lee still used her old log cabin kitchen for family gatherings. ..The cabin wasn't fancy but it had homed Anney Lee's brood.. The old cooking pots and tin pitchers and platters were there and was a tie to her Mother and grandmother who were gone by then ..many years. .But Anney felt a tie with her loved ones as she used their old cooking vessels. .

She never took to her new kitchen even after she was very old. .And was often found in her log cabin at supper time. Lighting a fire in the fire place and cooking a meal for her husband. As twilight came, Anney Lee would be found in her chair sitting by the fire thinking of the many family dinners of long ago. .The cabin was home to Anney Lee and she could never leave it. .her heart was there and remained there I guess until she drew her last breath.

I read another story years ago about a Mother who got a new stove back in the 40's I think. .And the family put her old cook stove in the basement. .They set it up to use for when they had company and to keep the basement warm. And every time the family went to visit the grandmother, they noticed how clean the new modern stove in the kitchen was. And come to find out, the grandmother never used it at all, as she didn't know how it worked. She did all of her cooking and baking on the old stove in the basement...

And I can't use a dishwasher. I don't know how it works. .I can't even stack the dishes in it. My sister- in- law laughed and laughed at me over Christmas as I was supposed to fill the dish washer at my folks house. .She wondered why I always washed the dishes in the sink. .And you should of seen me with the first Microwave we had. .I thought if the buzzer went off, then you had to get the food out in a hurry or it would blow up. .So when the buzzer went off, I am yelling like crazy for the kids as I wouldn't even open the door of it. .Mary wrote a story about it in the early 90's.. I should have her write something about me. You all would laugh your heads off.

60

Kitchen Klatter (Part 2)

I am getting ready to have Baby in about 15 minutes but wanted to write a few thoughts. .Ya know, this afternoon I was reading again those lil' housewife magazines. .And I just felt so sad. .A lot of the writings are the granddaughters describing the log cabins their grandmas had. .They had seen them first hand. .This was back in the 70's and the granddaughters were grandmas themselves. .And I remember as a child how sweet my grandparents were. .But then my own mother's generation lost a lot of that during the WW2 years. .So of course I feel cheated that not only did I not know a Mother who lived in a log cabin, but the relatives my mother's age think the whole idea stunk.. And if I feel cheated, you all must be mad as hell. . Ya know, we can thank feminism for all of this. .Even in the Kitchen Klatter magazines it was making its play for young Moms to hit the bricks and go to work.. I hate feminism now even more than I ever did after seeing what could have been; had so many women not bought into the biggest lie ever told...Satan hates we Marys and our seeds of Christ. And what better way can he buckle us than to tell us we ain't worth nothin' and our place at home is a joke. .It's no wonder so many of us feel like we are continually walking through a maze of evil spirits as we try to do the dishes or sweep the floor. . Getting a job is often a relief. .Feminism is an unholy stinkin' fire that is seeping into our homes and killing our children and our marriages.. And people worry about carbon monoxide poisoning..

The silent killer of feminism is invisible, and too bad we don't have an instrument to detect it.. Well we do - the Bible. .I always laugh as I see some woman, "Yes Sir" her boss. .She believes in submission, but not to her husband. .Or, "Yes Brother Bob I am happy to sing in the choir." ..Women are submissive creatures and she will submit to someone. .The sin is that she won't submit to her husband and her home duties. . She won't be a keeper at Home. .She is but a girl and not woman enough to stand for what is right and stand for God when the church ladies have gone home. .She serves the Lord as a man pleaser and cares not to please the Lord and Him alone. .Well Baby is about here so I better cool off.. take a deep breath and drink a lot of water. .When I talk about feminism, I get very distracted.

61

Mothers Prayers

I had told Jim in my bitterness.. "Well the unbelievers were right. .I should of just gotten a job and a career and forgotten about home school.. I knocked myself out raising my children for Jesus and now I have come to the same end as the whorish women. .What good did it do me to live for God?" And ya know, had a I stopped mid stream and quit prayin', it would have, I think, gone like that. .But I didn't give up and plan to never give up until I see my children all walkin' with the Lord. . . folks would say to me, early in my marriage. ."Why are you having all those kids, so you can get more welfare?" Oh it broke my heart what they said. .And, "Why are you wanting you husband to come back home? He will just leave again." And I would stand up to them and say, "My Children will not be a part of this world's problems ..they will be an answer and bring many to Christ." ..And then for Satan to supposedly prove to me that the unbelievers were right? But see if the devil is worried about you, he will always take you to this point. .He will show you that the lies said about you weren't lies, but truth. .And this is where you get down to a burning wire ..The devil just proved to you that you were an idiot for standing on God's word. And all the hecklers were right? And this is where a true believer stands up like Job and says, "Though He slay me, yet will I trust in Him." The dust has cleared and the so- called- truth arises, "You ARE the village idiot?" And if you are standing on what you can see and not believing in what you can't see, and God's word, then you will give up at this point. .

But if you are walking by what you believe, then you will leave the girls behind and go on in Him and just keep walkin'. And as you step into the supernatural power of God, He will delight in you and keep you walkin' on water. .He guides us to this place where all is lost in order to force us into the supernatural ..Because for some of us, we have gotten into problems that there is no answer in this world for. .And so we are forced by trial and error to step out of the boat and into the water. .We don't want to go as we feel we will drown. .But when we come to the end of ourselves, the miracles must come ..They have to as Jesus has promised that anything we ask in Jesus' Name, we will receive. .And it is not His will that any should perish. . So when we pray for someone to be saved, we have a right to expect this to happen. It is God's will and we can rest assured that it will happen come hell or high water. It has to come. .All it takes is prayer warriors to birth this into the physical realm. .And all the hecklers and godless about me can laugh at me and say that I shudda done this and that and been like them and lived in the world like they did. .But I am standing with my God and I believe He is a rewarder to those who diligently seek Him. Let God be God and every man a liar.. Walk by what you believe and not by what you see.. Get your eyes off the physical circumstances and onto His reality. .

He is the same yesterday today and forever. Don't give your life for a pot of porridge, or give up your life for this world's ideas. Stand up in Christ and be willing to die for Him. .Only what is done for Christ in this world will last. .Some day we will all be dust ..But will we leave behind a foot print in the sand? Godly boys and girls who, through Mothers tears, have been birthed unto Christ. .Can we leave a voice behind, dear Mothers. .A voice crying in the wilderness "Repent for the kingdom of heaven is at hand"..

62

Amazing Grace (Part 1) [9/12/05]

[Granddaughter, six week old, Baby Chloe Faye, died of crib death (on 9/7/05). She was the daughter of Brandon and Mary, Connie's youngest daughter.]

Yesterday morning was Baby's Funeral.. This morning I woke up with the weight of the world upon my chest. .I prayed, "Oh God how will I make it now for the rest of my life?" And the Lord speaks to my heart, "Neglect not the gift that is within you." And of course my gift is writing. It was the most spiritual and lovely funeral I have ever been to. Mary picked a little country graveyard ..Not far away was a fence with cows grazing peacefully. .Folks began to gather about the tent. .I saw our Christian Joy come over the hill and she took one look at the funeral and began to walk quickly the other way.. And then ran as hard as she could up to a grassy hill top. .I ran after her, calling her.. She fell upon the ground and wept and sobbed .."Mom I can't take it." My heart laid down with my precious daughter, age 31. I sat with her on the ground and rubbed her legs and feet and comforted her. .Mary saw her and came up to the hill top with us and ministered to our Christian

Joy. .her precious sister ..Our Mary was the rock as I knew she would be...

Chrissy got back up as Mary gave her a little job to do...In the service Mary sang a song I had made up. [Something I sang to Mary as a baby] ..called, "Baby Fat Cheeks" And Mary sang it to Chloe Faye as one last song before we had to say good bye to our darling baby. .Papa wrote a letter to her and read it. .At the end of the letter it read, ."Chloe Faye, Grandpa will see you someday soon, so make room for Grandpa in heaven." ...And afterwards Jim placed the letter in Baby's casket. .Others said farewell to Chloe Faye.. only 6 weeks old ..And yet huge in our lives and none of us will ever be the same. .Mary and Brandon had a wonderful service for their precious first born baby. . After the service, we all went up on a hill by the tent ..And Mary had white balloons with helium in them. .The family wrote letters to Chloe with black felt markers. .Mary tied her message balloon with Brandon's balloon and she let theirs go first and then the rest of us let our balloons go ..And in the background our friend Glenn played his bag pipes, "Amazing Grace." And oh our Savior's grace is amazing. .We watched the balloons fly away like white birds flying to heaven with a message. .There were about 20 balloons. .The sight was so breath taking ..so uplifting. .We are all forever changed by Chloe's life and death.. Later at a dinner, a dear friend told me, "Connie you should write a book" I said "I am .I am!!!" I would die of a broken heart if I didn't have the gift of writing. .And a writer must write. .God has a hold of my neck and it's write or

die. .Of course I would rather die. .But it is not my time to go
..and if I don't obey God, I will live to regret it. .I feel locked at
times in a basket hung over the edge. .I live on a branch that
hangs over troubled waters. .And on this branch the Lord has
called me to make a nest ..To not look down, to trust in God to
keep on goin' ..I feel like I am put together with paper clips
and scotch tape. And all my paper clips have sprung loose. And
what holds me back from falling over my cliff is one piece of
tape.. And yet God's amazing Grace keeps me. And He who
made us never slumbers nor sleeps. .He is with us always. .Yes,
He is amazing...Was His grace sufficient for me and my family
in this heartache and sadness? Yes His grace is sufficient...

63

His Mercy (Part 2)

I told Jim that if Rex, a friend of ours, knew that we had lost our grandbaby, he would be there at the funeral. .He did find out and was there. .When I saw him, I said, "Well there's old Calhoon ..I knew we would see you." He came over and hugged Jim and me ..This man is hands down the worst man I have ever known. ..And I have known some of the worst of 'em.. Take my word for it, this guy is something I can't even describe...But his wife Ruth won't let him go...She just keeps on praying and calls me on the phone to pray with her . .and I do. I have given up prayin' for this man who has brought heartache to 2 generations of his own family. .But when Ruth calls, I get back up and pray again...I have prayed that he would quit committing adultery. This guy is 62 yrs. old and still won't stop with the adultery. .His wife is a saint of God and a sister to me in Christ. .Calhoon. .not his real name . . comforted Jim and I at the funeral. .And if Jim and me don't look good to an old sinner like he is, then we don't look good to God. .

The way I figure it, Jim and I ain't nothin' but beggars ourselves. .But Rex sat with us and when Jim broke.. Rex got up and went over to Jim and held him. .He and his wife Ruth held me as I broke ..I looked into Rex's eyes and said, "You are acquainted with grief and you are touched by our hearts." ..If anyone thinks adultery is fun? Then you are a very misguided person. .You should see what it does to you over the long haul. .. it locks you solid into hopelessness . .It robs you of your soul. .And the Lord tells me to love Calhoon ..Me prayin' for judgment to burn his rear off ain't gonna do it. .Believe me, if it would have, this guy would have nothing to hold his pants up. .His wife and I have prayed for this guy for 25 years and he only has gotten worse. .

And yet God is God; and yesterday Jim and I applied our love again to him ..As Rex comforted us in our grief and his heart was open, Jim and I prayed silently that the Lord would set Rex free. Ruth stood and watched and prayed. .I have learned through this trial of my faith and praying with Ruth for Rex, that the Lord is so long suffering and merciful to us. . Oh we want to call down fire out of heaven for these sinners. . And yet God's timing is not ours. .Our days feel like years to us sometimes ..And yet a thousand years is like a day to Jesus. . No one is hopeless and the Lord will always forgive us. .As long as someone is alive, they can be forgiven. .Yet repentance must come before we can reach heaven for an eternity. .I do wonder at times if the Lord would have Ruth and I go to the this woman, who Rex commits adultery with, and become friends with her and lead her to Christ. .Well of course she goes to church . But evidently she doesn't know the Lord!! I mean, there is more than one way to skin a cat. .I mean something has to give here. .But one thing Rex told me just before they left to go home ..He looked into my eyes and he said, "Connie one good thing is that this baby will never know sin." ..I mean, I noticed everyone else had said to us, "This baby will never know sorrow and grief." ..But to Rex, sin was the most devastating thing he knew of. .And except for God's grace, we would all be adulterers. .I thank God that the Lord has redeemed Jim and me ..I thank the Lord that God is bringing my children to Christ. .We don't come to heaven by our good works but by His finished work on Calvary. .It's not all about us and what we do. .it is all about Him and His obedience to die for us.. He paid for our sins and, as we receive Him, we are forgiven.

64

God's People (Part 3)

Our dear friend Chuck preached the sermon for the funeral. .
Oh mercy he is white haired now with a white beard...Oh
where has the time gone? Chuck gave a salvation message and
an invitation to receive Christ. .He told about how I had won
him to the Lord in 1972....He said, "Out of Connie's grief she
spoke of Christ to me." I was a young wife deserted of my
husband. But the Lord had me to be a witness for Christ. .
Bonnie, a dear Christian friend, brought Chuck to my house. .
My lil' Jimmy Mike, my only child, was asleep in bed. .
Everyone had given up on Chuck. He was 24 yrs old... Bonnie's
Dad wouldn't even let Chuck in the living room . . Bonnie's
Mom, a dear Christian, called every day begging me to pray
that Bonnie would not marry Chuck. . Of course I didn't want
her to marry him either. Chuck was a biker and a drug addict
and alcoholic. .But Bonnie brought him over to my house. .
And I figured, ya know? I can't hurt this poor bum any by
telling him about Jesus. .I was 22 years old. .So I went ahead
and told him about the saving grace of Jesus.. And a power hit
Chuck and nearly knocked him off his chair.. The last thought

he had before he received the Lord was, "How can I get out of here? Where's the back door? " And after that, he entered the kingdom of God. .His rotten career of drug abuse was over in an instant. .That night he laid down the drugs and alcohol and picked up the Bible and couldn't get enough of it. .He still drives a Harley ..but has won many to Christ Jesus. He and Bonnie did marry and together have known the Lord for many years. Their son is a wonderful preacher and their daughter a precious stay at home Christian Mother. They are a dear family. .Chuck is a popular Bible teacher in our area. .Chuck laid down the drugs and picked up another spirit ..The spirit of Jesus Christ.. He loved the word of God the first night he was saved. .

Bonnie didn't know what to think of him. .No one did. .it seemed almost scary ..How could a man be droppin' acid and drinkin' beer like water, all of a sudden lay all that down and pick up the Bible and read nothing but that? Chuck loved the word of God like no one I have ever seen.. It was as though he poured the word of God all over his sins. .And all the hurt and wounds were drowned in the water of life. .The word of God is a healing for all of our afflictions and our sins. .I am so amazed at how short life is. .It seems so long as we live it but it's over in such a short time. Just give your lives to Jesus, dear Mothers. .Just put Him first. Don't waste your lives on the world.. Stay home and connected to the family and to the Lord. .So now as our family lives these next days without our baby Chloe, we are the walking wounded. .Our hearts forever severed waiting for the healing oil of Christ to mend us..

Every time Mary breaks down I hold her and tell her.. "Mary. . . I PROMISE.. I promise you will get over the hurt and it will be less and less each day". .And Mary nods her head, yes, in silence. .Yesterday Mary was so peaceful ..She said, "Mom I feel guilty that I am not crying." I said, "No Mary the Lord has His arms around you. .Accept His love." Brandon went back to work today. .May the Lord give him strength. .All is well ..all is well. .God has us in His hands ..And now it is time to rebuild the walls and make it as safe again as it can be. .The Lord speaks to my heart. "Connie all is well ..rebuild the wall .and make a home a safe place of refuge again."

65

Papa's Roses (Part 1)

So yesterday the rest of the out- of- town kids left. Just
before John and Christine.. his wife left, Mary asked us, "Do
you all want to go out to the cemetery to see the cross Brandon
made for the baby? " Well it was very late and we all knew that
by the time we got out there, that it would be pitch dark. And
yet Mary and Brandon were grieving and so we all said we
would go out. .Papa had bought a half dozen more dark pink
roses for Mary...In the dark of the graveyard, Mary put the
roses around the wooden cross that Brandon had made, as it
stuck out of the ground at Baby's gravesite. .Mommy and
Daddy— to Chloe Faye, sat with a flash light crumpled on the
ground somehow making up Baby's bed for the night. .

And this morning I awoke not hurting as much as I had. .
knowing we all must go on in Jesus. .The Lord gives me the
scripture as I awoke this morning." He gives us beauty for
ashes; the oil of Joy for mourning; the garments of praise for
the spirit of heaviness. We are the trees of righteousness, the
plantings of the Lord and Jesus is glorified. .I just wrote that
from the memory of it in my heart. .I hope it is right. .How
many times I have had to take on the garments of praise? And

I know, as a seasoned believer, that He gives us beauty for ashes and the oil of joy for mourning. .Yes Jesus is still on the throne. .

Ya know, Emily ..Dixie's daughter, is a precious saint of God. She is 28.. I think or right at that age? .Her Mama Dixie died about 3 yrs. ago. .Emily told Jill she had a vision of her Mother just lately. .Em didn't know whether to tell our family about it or not ..But Jill encouraged Em to tell us. Emily said to me at the cemetery. ."Connie I had a dream of Mom. .And she said, "It's all right. Baby Chloe Faye is in heaven with me. .Don't worry about it." I asked Emily to tell Mary. .And when Em started to tell Mary ..Mary said a peace just came over her, even before Em finished telling her ..When Emily said those few sentences, we all felt such an anointing come upon us. . Like the Lord had anointed us with His truth.. Heaven? Oh I dunno. I guess I have thought of it a lot over the years ..But heaven is a different place to me now ..It's more real. I don't know everything about it. .But I know Dixie went there and Chloe Faye.. And I know that Dixie would help God watch over our Baby there. I just know Dixie.. and I know she wouldn't let anything happen to our baby girl. .

I do search the scriptures for references on heaven. It seems my heart has swung open to a feeling of heaven that I can't explain. .I know my heart is partly with Baby in heaven and partly with Mary on earth. .But ya know, Dixie would never flinch and was always so matter of fact. I can see her in heaven even now with the angels caring for Baby ..Papa also got a half dozen red roses to put on the baby's casket to stand between her and the soil. Mary told the undertaker, "Now we want these flowers to be on top of the casket. .And Mary laid wild flowers on the casket too and Brandon's Mom laid wild flowers ..And yes we know that the Rose of Sharon - Jesus Christ is with our baby. .Again Papa planted the Rose of Sharon bushes at the side of our house last spring and they are all in bloom now. .And I think of the wilderness rose that blooms in a dry and thirsty land. .I think of how the Lord gives us miracles in the place where no other miracles have bloomed before. .I feel the presence of angels as I write. .

And I said to God last night, "Lord how will I live from now on. .I feel so fearful." .And the Lord said to me, "Connie I know that and I will help you over this." I think we feel so condemned if we don't have faith all the time. .But ya know what? We are just human beings? God knows we are made of the dust? I am His girl and He will care for me and my children. He would have to.

66

Courage (Part 2)

Oh mercy. Yesterday a dear friend came over to see me. .I will call her Beth. .not her real name. .She brought a present for Mary and a card. .We get together about once or twice a year. .Many years ago I told her about Jesus at the welfare office. We often laugh and laugh over that. .The story goes like this: Jim had left me for about the 20th time and I had to go get Welfare as I was high and dry with about 3 kids at the time. . . God knows I had to feed them. .Anyway I had this little book called, "Victory over Circumstances." And I had purposed in my heart to read that dang thing, 'cause I sure needed victory over circumstances. Oh Yeah!!!! And I figured I would read it while I waited to be called in by the social worker. All I wanted was to be quiet and read. .But this lady next to me, who I didn't know at the time, kept asking me what time it was and different things ..I kept praying,"Lord tell this woman to get lost or something, I am trying to get some victory goin' on here." Well I know that was a terrible thing to say to the Lord but it's the truth.. My heart was ripped up inside and I didn't want to talk to anyone. .But you know, this lady kept asking me questions and buggin' me. .So I got creative and I thought,

I bet if I ask her if she is saved she will think I am a religious zealot and leave me alone. .

So I asked her if she knew Jesus and if she was saved and on her way to heaven.." Well she said, "Yes I am saved." And I said, "No you aren't." I know that was rude and I don't know why I said it just out like that. Well I ended up giving her my phone number. .And later she went home and in the privacy of her bedroom she got on her knees and she said, "Lord I thought I was saved and on my way to heaven.. If I am not saved, then please tell me and show me how to receive Christ." . . Beth said that the room filled with a golden light and the Lord spoke to her heart and she received Jesus into her heart. . And this was about 35 years ago. .Beth is now 67. .She has won many to Christ. .I am ashamed to say that she almost had to buy the information from me on how to get saved. .God forgive me. .Talk about an unwilling vessel?

Beth had a husband that was the limit. .But the Lord delivered him from alcoholism about 23 years ago. One time, in a drunken rage, he got out all of his guns and laid them on the table in Beth's kitchen. ."Which one do you want me to shoot you with? " He said. .Well what a question hu? Beth remained silent and he picked up a gun and shot it through the wall. Then he left the house.. Beth went over to the table and got the guns. . put them back on the rack. .Took a picture and nailed it over the gunshot on the wall and went back to her baking and cooking. She had 3 children to feed and care for. . That woman never missed a beat. .no kidding.. What a saint of

God. .And play the guitar? Oh my ..what a wonderful musician!! And everywhere she goes, miracles follow her..

And ya know, My friend and neighbor, Char ..oh what a joy she is. .Char came from a loving Catholic Irish background. . She is a Baptist now. .But so many of her ways reflect the old time Catholic Mothers. Char says that often her aunts would talk to her with their hand over their heart. .They were so compassionate with many children to care for. Char asked her aunt Mary when her husband had died? .She assured her that she would have come to the funeral had she known. .Aunt Mary says, "Would you like a piece of pie?". . Finally Char got it out of this dear saint that yes, her husband had died. .But Aunt Mary put others before herself. .She ministered first to those around her. .And now following her example of courage. . . and in the worst of times ..Miss Charlotte and I will say, "Would you like a piece of pie?" Oh yes we go on and we live in His anointing ..In His bubble of trust. .He comes and walks with us in our furnace of affliction.

67

The Church at Home

Dear Christian Mothers, Your faithfulness will be rewarded by the Lord. .For He rewards those who diligently seek Him. . As you have suffered, planting precious seeds .. you will come again rejoicing bringing in the sheaves. .As you have suffered and died with Him, you will be raised up again almost like from the dead. .and you will live to see His glory. .You will see your children come to Christ and live for Christ. .You gave them a truly Christian home. .They had a mother who rose early to seek the Lord. .And she never gave up on her husband through it all. .And he will know the Lord too. .They will remember Mother whose faith weathered the storm ..You will become dear to them as they get older and remember your faith . .And how they gave up on themselves and yet Mother never gave up; although she was the one who was hurt the most by their backslidings.. Even now, as I write I am crying and yet would my writing touch your heart for God had I not known the grief I speak of? The disappointments? And the children we cry over the most are the ones who will do the most for God. .

But just because your family isn't like maybe what the teachers out there say is: "The perfect Christian family," Don't give up, you'll have a truly Christian home . .I mean most families aren't perfect no matter how much we wish they were. . . Life is always a process.. Just because your children ain't perfect at 18, that doesn't mean you failed. .They will all know the Lord, but maybe not in your timing. .We can plant a seed but we can't make it grow.

Last night as Char {My neighbor} and I visited, she said, "Connie, Jim is a miracle...it's a miracle how the Lord has kept all of your family.." And it is. . Chrissy calls from NYC. "Mom someday a movie will be made of our lives as a family" ..My life here with my family has been a faith adventure. .Our oldest, Jimmy, age 37, travels all over the world doing light designs for on-stage plays. .Christian Joy is now getting famous as a clothes designer. .Johnny, at one time, had his own radio show. .And then Dan thinks he is Elvis and plays in a band.. Mary and David are more quiet. .thank God. .and Jim just walks around being a living, breathing miracle.. All he has to do is get up in the morning and he makes a statement. .And Mama keeps on praying and being obedient to her calling as Keeper at Home. .

Often I hear vibrations around me. .I know someday my family will break this world wide open for Christ. .I just have a knowin' in my heart. .I don't know when or how, but it's comin'. . Because I live from my visions, from within, I can enjoy each of my children in the stages they are in. .Each coming to Christ, as He leads them many times through the valley of the shadow of death. .I often walk with them and I cry out, "Lord save us lest we die." And I let them go as much as I can . . And I watch them from the ground as they play upon the rugged cliffs and laugh at danger. .I cry out to God, "Lord watch them and keep them as the apple of thine eye." And I awake in the night and cry out to God as the fear grabs my soul and Satan tells me that my children are all worldly and will never be anything for Jesus. And yet the Lord weaves my prayer cloth when I don't know how. .And I step back and He weaves on. .And my tears stain His hands and He works a design that I had never understood. .And it is glorious and it will win many to His heart. .Only He knows how to call and woo His own to His side. .Only He can create a clean heart and convict the soul of the lost. .This mother I am describing to you, it is a normal Christian mother who is building a normal Christian Home. .

Most of what we see in Christiandom is not always what we think it is. .But the true way to Christ comes the hard way from many tears of the intercessor. .Maybe it is the Father who prays ..But more often it is the praying Mother who builds the home with her silent, godly prayer and works.

68

Mother's Place

Speaking of eating dessert before you are supposed to, My Great Grandpa Canaday always sat down to the table and ate his dessert first. .Then he would eat the rest of the meal. .But his dessert always came first. Can't ya just see the children at the table wanting their dessert first? Great Grandpa lived with his son and family so there were children around. .But ya know, back then the men were honored at the table and what they did, the children knew they wouldn't get away with. .My Mom, as a child, would sneak food over to her mother's plate that she didn't want to eat. .Because back in the old days, during the Depression era, it was a sin if you left food on your plate . .

I remember my Mother's Mother always saying her favorite piece of the chicken was the neck. .I could never figure that out until I became a mother of many children. .My Grandmother said that, as that was probably the only piece of chicken left by the time she was done serving everyone else and got to eat herself. .The old time mothers were so holy back then. I mean you didn't allow anyone to cuss in front of your mother.. When my mom would get with her other 5 siblings, they would speak of the everyday things that happened in their families. .And many, many times, I heard them say, "Oh don't tell Mom." Ya know, the old time mothers were protected by the husband, and even the children seemed to protect her. .

My Gram babysat for my brother and me in our home for about a year. That woman wouldn't have worn lipstick if you gave her a million dollars. . She would wear bracelets or a necklace to church ..Earrings ..oh no!!! She wouldn't have drank an alcoholic drink for all the tea in China. . She wouldn't even drink soda pop. . She drank tea or water with a meal. .She taught me to sew the little stitches. And as I see Christian Joy's hand sewing, it is just as I taught her, and as Gram taught me..

But here is a funny story. .My Aunt Lilly was such a hoot, I will never forget her.. She was Mother's sister. .Well when I was about 20 yrs. old, we were at a family get- together at one of the uncle's house. Well Aunt Lilly was having nervous problems and she wanted to smoke a cigarette. .Well she had smoked for 30 yrs., but never in front of her mother. .Well Gram knew Lilly smoked, but had never seen her out and out with a cigarette in her mouth. .So we are all in the living room. . . And off the living room was this closet with a curtain drawn over it. . So Lilly went behind this curtain and got a chair and decided to smoke this cigarette trying to hide from her mother. . . I mean Lilly is grown and married and is about 50 years old at the time. Gram is standing outside the curtained door and the smoke is just roaring over the top of the curtain. .Everyone is looking at Gram to see what she will say. .Gram is watching the smoke roar over the top of the door. She isn't saying anything but Lilly can see from under the curtain, as she sees her Mom's black shoes and that Gram is standing right outside the door. .Pretty soon Lilly cries out. ."I haven't smoked in front of my mother in 30 yrs., and I don't plan on starting now." And that whole scene will tell ya a lot. I mean a Mother back then was put on a pedestal. .She was like the family conscience. .None of her daughters would dare smoke a cigarette in front of their mother. .Father was head of the house ..the undisputed head. .And Mother was the moral compass.. Mother sat in a place of dignity and honor. .

Now my Gram would never even say "shoot." She thought that was a dirty word. .Even my own mother.. I had never heard say a dirty word until I was 12 yrs old. .Mom said "Shoot," and we thought that was getting near the edge. .But when I was 12, I wanted to make sandwiches for the neighborhood. .I told Mom I needed 12 pieces of bread. And Mom said, "12 pieces of bread my butt." And that was such a shock I never forgot it and that has been about 40 some years ago..

69

Spiritual Battles

We are called to be helpers. .We are called to make a platform of rest and peace so that our husbands can be priest of the home. .He shouldn't have to worry about us, or if we are doing right with the children. .Or if we are running around when they are at work. .We should be wives that bring our husbands great rest and peace.. They should trust us and feel that we are responsible Mothers and wives at home. This platform of peace gives a man the confidence to run the home and go to work. .We are called as helpers. We are called to fit into our husband's lives.

See when I was young, I didn't want to do Christmas. .I thought it was a pagan holiday, and I would fight Jim on it. . Well good night that caused all kinds of problems. .Finally I submitted to him. .Jim had wonderful memories of old fashioned Christmases of long ago, when he was a young boy. . So I just decided that I would make our Christmases old fashioned too, and that I would join into the Christmas Spirit. Of course the children loved it ..I had to learn to fit in with my husband. .

I love the house to be quiet.. But Papa would invite an alligator for lunch if he thought I wouldn't notice it...So I have to get to rock and rollin' in my kitchen and scare up some grub. .Even if it is for a person I would rather not even know . . let alone fix lunch for. .But I am Jim's helper .. I am not his guide. And now -a-days, a lot of the time Papa will ask my opinion. .As I don't try to boss him, he feels free to ask me what I think. .But if I get on my high horse and try to run the show, then he clams up. .But see, if things ain't goin' right here at the house? The Lord wants me to pray about it. .Sometimes Papa doesn't get the hrs. at work? And he works less? This drives me up the wall. .It interrupts my authority in my home.. I have a place where I hold absolute authority and that is as helper and keeper at home. .Sometimes I need to take the time out to pray, and the heck with the dishes. .But when Jim is around, I have to keep movin' and serving the family. .So I need my place in God to regroup and to take charge in my place of duty. .So if Jim doesn't get enough hours, then I pray and God gives him the hours he needs.

See my place of obedience is important too. .And when we go before God, dear saints, we come "Not" as wives and mothers to a family. .We come as daughter of the most High God. .In God there is no male or female. .We can come boldly to the throne of grace. .We have authority in God...But we will get struck down by Satan if we go to rebuking demons with no covering on our heads.. And I mean spiritual coverings of our obedience to our husbands as unto the Lord. .We enter God's throne room with a spirit of submission to our husbands ..And as we talk with God, we go into the spirit and this is where we are His daughters ..But we have to come to God with the covering of our husbands.. .It's called bowing to the Lord?

See if you are watching lady preachers on tv, you are filling your spirit with witchcraft. .Rebellion is the same as witchcraft. . If you see one of those women come on tv, you should run like heck to get away from her. .She will serve you up in hell like a roasted goose. .That woman spells trouble with a capital "T". .She is against all that is stable and orderly in the Home...She may sound pretty at first? But let her teachings come deep within you to your inner woman? She will dig out of you the meek and quiet spirit and will cause your home to split up. .No, not at first she won't. .But she will in the end. . Just wait until those seeds she is planting takes root, and then begin to spread their seeds? They are vipers eggs that WILL hatch and not only ruin your family, but the families you influence for evil...No, don't feel that because you aren't top banana that you aren't important ..It's just that you are the weaker vessel and you are easily bruised..

70

Adultery (Part 1)

Dear Ladies, Good Morning!!! Jim went to play golf this morning, and I don't have the Baby. .It is so peaceful and quiet in the house this morning. .I am so anxious to do my writing and so wanting to do my homemaking too...Oh sweet peace when it is quiet in the house. .Such a rare and delicious time for a busy homemaker, Mother and Grandmother. .Yesterday as I went about my business, I kept getting glimpses of Wisdom. .I could see huge trees bowing over me. .The branches were thick and heavy...I could see them protecting my house ..As the Lord showed me this, I could feel my chest loosen up as the stress of life had me down. Also, in the eye of the storm it is quiet and still. .And around the eye is a whipping noisy wind. . strong and powerful. .Lately as I live, I see so many in such a tumultuous wind and yet I feel protected and peaceful. .

Yesterday I turned on the tv and I caught a minute at the end of this minister's sermon...One of his closing sentences was, "If you don't kill what is after you, and that God has called you to kill ..it will kill you." Man that was powerful to me. .And I think of how my own home in the old days nearly killed me.. And yet I didn't give up; and the Lord used me to kill what was trying to kill me. .And now my dear husband, who was nearly the ruin of me, protects me like an angel so I can minister to others. And that's how God works. .He doesn't stick a battle in front of you to destroy you, but to give you victory. .Forget the, "Why did this happen to me?" Take up the whole armor of God and go after the devil who is out to kill you ..

Ladies, hey guess what? We live in an adulterous sin- sick society. .Some lil' Sunday School lesson about Noah ain't gonna save you from the devil. .You better get on your knees and learn how to intercede in prayer. .It's called work, and you can't do it as you go for a walk, or watch tv., or do something else. .You have to get ahold of God and fast and pray, and it may take years before you see His glory.. So count the cost: Do you want to go? Or do you want to stay home? Are you willing to give up your precious reputation and get out of your comfort zone? Are you gonna let the devil have you, or are you gonna have the devil and be a testimony for God? Ya got a choice. Ya wanna be killed, or kill the evil in your life? We are living in hard times. .oh yeah .. You don't have time to fool around ..And ya know, Mary L. my mentor, used to tell me, when I would tell her I was scared to death.. She would say, "Connie the fearful and the adulterers will not enter into the kingdom of God." In other words, ladies, the fear will send ya to hell. .And Hell is a real place. .Now the church ladies like to say how scared they are of everything. .and they tell me, "Well

Connie you are naturally not afraid of anything." How ignorant for them to say that to me. .I told them I get plenty scared, but I am not afraid enough to quit. .Fear is a natural thing, but it's what ya do with it that counts. .

Some of you need to just get down with God and vow that you will make a home for your children no matter what your husband does. .If he is off runnin', let him go. .The children need to be cared for. .And you should be woman enough to protect the children, and to keep all of the ugly truth away from them. They are children ..give them a life...I raised my first 3 children under stress that was unreal. .For 12 yrs., I had to make a home under pressure ..I mean, you all will never know the half of it. .Jimmy, our oldest son, said he never knew anything was goin' on. If I could help it, I never said a cross word in front of the children to Jim. .The children need to feel safe and should not have to bear the fear themselves. .And as I tell you to go ahead and make a home for the children, no matter what, I say this as one who has been there and done that. .Walk out each day in God, and don't look at the adultery and the sin. .Your husband will pay for his own sins.

71

Homemaking (Part 2)

Ya know, in the old days, Dixie would tell me when I was in a tight spot. Which was often, by the way.."Connie, are you into your homemaking?" I hated it when she said that to me, as I was thinkin', "How does she think all this stuff gets done if I wasn't doin' it?" But she meant creative homemaking, not just picking up messes. .She would tell me, "Connie, the homemaking spirit will break the power over Satan. It will break his back." And ya know, yes we have to pray and give the night to prayer as Jesus did. .But then the next day, we do the works of righteousness.. We sleep at night, when we can. We go in and out of sleep as we pray and read the word. But then the next day, we get up to do the works of God. .We must be about our Fathers business.. We, as Mothers, must be duty bound and able to maintain a pattern of good works in our work places - our homes....Maybe ya don't feel like fixin' supper, but ya better get at it. The family needs you and it's a blessing for you to get in your kitchen and to do your homemaking. .Faith without works is dead. .We must put legs onto our faith and prayers ..We have to do more than pray and seek the Lord. We must cook and clean and tend to the business of our homes..

I just stopped here to make some banana bread and some "Wash Day " Soup. .I had a half a small beef roast in the freezer. .And as I remember that meat was as tough as a shoe. . So I am boiling it with some tomatoes and onions and a pkg. of gravy mix. .salt and pepper. . When it's half done, I will cut it in cubes and cook it some more with some potatoes and other veggies. Papa will love it.. Also, I thought I had a recipe for banana bread, but didn't . ."Well I don't know where it is." So I just threw in a big bowl, some self rising flour and the last of the biscuit mix, with some shortening and some bananas, and spices and brown sugar, and milk and eggs. It's in the oven now and I should rock and roll and get myself dressed and a bath taken while all that is baking and simmering on the stove. The house smells good.. All is well.

72

Winter Meals for Large Families (Part 1)

Dear Mothers ..Well the cold weather is settling in for our state of Iowa. .We have had about 3 nights where the temp. dropped to freezing. .Papa and me are slowly closing the home down for the cold weather . .I was thinking yesterday of how hard it was to keep up with my large family meals during the fall and winter months. In the summer it was easy as I had my garden and someone was always unloading fresh produce at my door, as they had more than they could use in their own gardens. .But mercy, when the cold months were upon us, it got hard. .I was so busy with babies and it was hard to grow enough food for the winter, and can it, etc. My neighbor next door said that she could hardly believe all the work I did. .

She and I really never knew each other until the children all grew up. I had to work like a dog and I loved it and would love to do it again. .it was a time of happy fruitfulness for me. .I was never really strong physically. .But I did what I could to keep the family goin' ..I homeschooled the youngest 3 and the older 3 went to public school. .for a time.. But here are some thoughts . .Ya know, when feeding a huge family like this, you

have to have a different mind -set than most small families..
The grocery store is designed to feed small families. .Like most
pkg. mixes are for 4 people, or at the most 6. .so forget that. .I
mean a box of pancake mix is gonna last you, what? 2
breakfasts? Every winter I would make up the Bisquick mix
using 5 pounds of flour. .And this would last me about 3
weeks. .I made pancakes with this nearly every day ..And often
I ran out of syrup and made my own ..In the fall, I would take
like 2 cups of apple cider and put it in a sauce pan. .I would
add about a Tbs. of cornstarch and brown sugar. . about 1 cup..
Then I would add cinnamon and start stirring until it boiled. .
If it is too thick, add a bit of water. And sometimes I made this
with Jello and sometimes with just water and brown sugar. .
But one of those lil' dinky bottles of syrup won't go far with a
large family. .I made a lot of rhubarb jam in the summer and
often the children put this on their pancakes.. But to try to
keep a whole houseful of children in cold, sugary cereal is
expensive. .But think about buying huge bags of flour and rice
and oatmeal. .And try your hand at making ketchup,
mayonnaise, syrup, and jams ..If you can make enough bread
and butter pickles and jams for the winter table, this is a lot. .

For any of you who have green tomatoes right now? You can
just pickle them. .Just slice them up thin with onions and
green peppers. .Then make up a recipe of 1 part white vinegar
and 1 part sugar. .boil this and pour this in the jar of sliced
vegetables. .Now you could add dill or garlic. . whatever ya
like. .Now, I know some of the family won't like pickled green

tomatoes but maybe some will. .And if no one likes them, just put the mixture in your blender and make a pickle relish out of it and use it in potato salad. Mother, you have to hide this stuff sometimes. .the kids eat it all so fast they don't know their potato salad has green tomatoes in it. .Another thing I used to do is buy big turkeys ..not just on the holidays. I would bake a turkey and freeze it in portions. .I would make a chicken soup with turkey. .If ya call it turkey soup the family may not eat it. . But I would put chicken flavorings in it, and my family didn't know the difference. And ya know, when my family was young, I made a homemade soup about every day. .Then if one of the older children got home late from their part- time, after school jobs, then there was always soup on the stove. .Or if one of the children didn't like what I was having for a main meal, there was soup. .I made a lot of chili and vegetable beef soups and potatoes soup was a favorite. .But the old time mothers always had a soup pot goin', on their stoves. .Like save all of your leftover veggies in a jar in the freezer for winter soups..

73

Winter Family Meals (Part 2)

Now in our area right now it is a good time to buy Potatoes and squash and pumpkins. .They are all reasonably priced. . Most of the time you can buy the big bags of potatoes for cheaper, per pound than the smaller bags. .And ya know, I used to use my front closed in porch for like a 2nd refrigerator in the winter. I would store milk out there. Then for a cool place for potatoes, I used my laundry room off the kitchen. I have a pantry back there too. .But in your home, you probably have places to store potatoes where they won't spoil. .I have my root cellar too and I put much of my home canned things down there. .And also at times I used the cake mixes ..They make the big cakes and in a pinch, they worked well for us. . But Mothers, if you can really discipline yourselves to getting up early and making pancakes or oatmeal for the family, this will make 'em happy and save on the grocery bill.. And then after breakfast, just start your bread for the day. .

When the hamburger was high priced, I would buy ground turkey and mix it with ground beef.. I used this mixture for chili and beef soups and many casseroles. .I would take my big cast iron Dutch oven and put a few pounds of ground turkey in it and hamburger. I would fry it up and add onions and spices. . . After it was done and cooled, I would pkg. this in small pkgs. for the freezer. .Ground turkey is so cheap and I think you can buy it by the box cheaper. .Also, many years ago I got a 2nd-hand freezer. .When this went out a few yrs. back it was like losing an old friend. .It was huge and I could store gallons of milk in it. .I used to pray when I went into the grocery store and I would ask the Lord to show me the buys. .And a lot of time I would happen upon dairy products that were almost outdated. .I would buy it all up and bring it home and freeze it. . . Well many times the kids would drink the milk up before the date was up. .I made a lot of yogurt and used it in place of sour cream or buttermilk. .or we just ate it with fruit...So when the cream was on sale, I would buy it up for 25 cents a half pint and made yogurt with it. I made it in a big stone crock. .David just loved it with a bit of sugar on the top. .it was rich and thick. .I made cream cheese with it too. But ya know, if you can just get up early and start your baking early before you start school, then this is a good thing. .I would have my children pretty much underway for school about 10:00 a.m ..I got them up at 6:00 and they had chores to do and had to get dressed and cleaned up. .And then by 7:30, we had devotions together and sometimes we did history together in the lower grades. . Then I would help them with some things like math and usually by 10:00, I was back to the kitchen. .The children had to keep the living room and dining room vacuumed. .they took turns. .And their beds had to be made before we started school. .I rarely did dishes as they had to do them ..they took turns. .But I had to cook and bake or we wouldn't have had any meals. .And I never wanted my children to think that we didn't have the food they needed. .I mean sometimes the children made cookies or helped with the cooking. But I was the one who mainly did the cooking and baking. .

And as the children got older and were in High school, I had to study to keep up with them. .But I had to put my heart into the kitchen and into praying to stay ahead of the meals. .If I got low on milk for the children, I would mix the whole milk with instant. .half and half. .They didn't know the difference unless they saw me mix it. .So I did a lot of this on the sly. .I made loads of bread puddings for desserts. .and cake puddings from leftover cake..

74

Large Families (Part 3)

And ya know, when the children are being schooled at home, you have to give them 3 good meals a day. .it isn't like when they went to Public school where they get a hot lunch.. heck some mothers send their children for breakfast too. .Well if ya have to, I guess it's better than nothing. But if your family is all home all day then you gotta really cook or go broke on buying mixes. .I think too what the Lord is telling me to say is that. .I cooked on purpose? It wasn't something I did once in a while or off the cuff? It was what I mainly did to put food on the table. .I gleaned and rummaged and prayed for food for the family. .It was my occupation. .See if Papa and me were out doing errands with the children on a Saturday or whatever. . We didn't have the option to go to the McDonalds on the way home. .So on a Saturday morning, I was up early before we left with the family and I had soup goin' for when we got back home.. One big meal the family loved was this. .I took my big turkey roaster and filled it with vegetables and fried hamburger and tomato soup. .and I would cook it on low all night. .The children would smell it in the night and could hardly wait to eat it for noon lunch. .I would turn if off the next morning but then I would heat it up just before we ate it. I always felt such satisfaction as I had things made ahead for my family to eat. .I mean I could have complained and came home to a cold house and stove and said, "Well if we could just go to McDonalds once in awhile, it would be nice." ..But I didn't want to complain. .I figured Papa was doing his best to support us and I wanted to do my part too. .I wanted my children to depend on Mother for what they ate. I didn't let my children hang at the Quick Trip. When they got hungry they thought of Mother and home and what was going on at home. .

Once I made a huge batch of vegetables with macaroni and fried meat, herbs, and tomato soup ....Johnny's wife says she will never forget that meal. I made it when she came to visit before they were married. .and I had so little to cook with. Most of the children were still home. .But Christine still remembers that meal ..it was wholesome and good and brought the family together in love and happiness. .It was a warm meal ..prayed over and put together with joy. . "Christine". .John's wife.. would sneak in the kitchen and eat it when no one was lookin'. .Well I had made plenty, so I didn't care. .Christine is a skinny lil' thing ..cute as a button. .and the mother of my first grandson, Romeo Paul. .But good food and plenty of it, is a blessing to a family ..it's worth the work and prayer. .

Papa has never turned anyone away from our table ..He just figures Mama has made enough to go around. .And this was a burden I kept to myself. .I just never wanted my family to think we didn't have enough food for what we needed. .I mean, with all the other hardships a family goes through, they deserve, at the end of the day, to have a warm meal and a cheerful and happy mother to put it on the table. .Whatever it takes, dear Mothers ..If ya need to go to the library and get some back- to- the- land cook books, then do it. .But don't serve your family with a stingy hand or naggy mouth. . Serve them with gladness and prosperity in your heart.

When I didn't have milk for the children, I gave them, "Fancy water," out of my best crystal glass pitcher ..All it was ..was water with ice in it. .But I served it with love to a family that took first place in my heart. .Papa prayed over it and thanked the Lord for it. .And the children thought they were served an expensive beverage. .it's all in the presentation, Dear hearts. Serve your family as you would the Lord, with a Joyful heart and the family will receive your ministry with Joy and gladness, peace, and a warm contentment..

75

Keepin' House (Part 1)

Dear Keepers at Home. .Ya know last night I was prayin' and
writing on paper. .Jim was watching TV and I had out my
paper, sitting on the couch.. I put some housewifery ideas on
paper and was prayin' and writing down my prayers too.. I
thought of the homemaking spirit and how if it isn't written
down, it would be lost. Of course you won't hear about it on tv,
or in most churches. .So unless it is hand- fed to some of you
..ya won't catch it. .and thank God for the many writers on the
internet who write about homemaking. .I love "Laine's"
writings and some of the other writings ...Before I write
further, I wanted to answer Nancy's email about needing
simple meal ideas.. Nancy you were talking about making
bread. Well you said you had a bread machine and that would
be a great help with the 4 extra children. .I would sure use it
and then maybe later on this fall learn to make it from scratch.
. . I would sure put the children to work too to help with the
homemaking. .I used to stand our children on a chair, up to
the sink and have them do dishes when they were about 3 or 4.
. . They make a mess, but they do get some dishes washed and

they learn how to help ..I mean make it safe for them, and put all the sharp stuff away. I wanted to tell you a few simple meal ideas. Aunt Toot had 7 children and I had 6, and we used to exchange meal ideas. .One thing we did is we made a lot of meals with the boxed mac. and cheese especially in the summer. .Just take a box of the mac. and cheese and make it as usual, then add a can of mixed vegetables and a can of cream of something soup. Or just the mix and a can of soup and extra cheese. .Just stir it all up and cook it until it bubbles. Toot used to put a can of already- made chili in hers with extra cheese.. And ya know, back in the old days, hot dogs were all meat and a better product than today. .Also baloney was all meat and very good. My grandmother used to fry baloney in the morning for breakfast and make fried potatoes with it. .

One meal I fixed a few days ago that was old fashioned and Papa loved, went like this: I got out my big cast iron skillet and put some grease in it. .Then I took a pound of hot dogs and fried them in the skillet. After they were brown, I put in my beans that I had mixed with ketchup and mustard and brown sugar. .I drain the pork and beans first and then add about a half cup of brown sugar, and a squirt of mustard and about a forth cup of ketchup ..I was using 2 cans of pork and beans drained and rinsed. .I don't leave all the goo on them. So anyway, after I put all this together, I laid some onions on the top and a slice of green pepper.. Then I baked this all in the oven until it bubbled and was browned...It was very good and Papa ate it as leftovers. And Jim isn't one to eat a lot of leftovers. .but he loved this dish. Now if your family likes onions and peppers, then you could fry them up, along with the hot dogs. But Jim doesn't like to eat onions. .So I just put a few in, big slices on the tops of my casseroles, to get an onion and pepper flavor. .My Jim loves black pepper, the coarsely ground kind. And I get that at the dollar store sometimes or I buy it at the Amish store.. I had put a lot of the black pepper in the beans I made. .And ya know, back in the old days, the mothers made lots of fried potatoes, often fried with onions. . Just get out a big skillet and put some grease in it and start slicing potatoes in the pan. .Have your flame up high and just slice more potatoes in as the others cook. After they are all browned, put a lid on them and a bit of water and let them simmer and get done. Kim said to just turn them once when ya think they are really crisp. .Even if they all stick together ..Kim is such a good cook and that is a good tip and has helped me to get better fried potatoes.

76

Keepin' House (Part 2)

Another thing we did with fried potatoes was when they were done, we would scramble up eggs with them and fry them until they were done. .It makes the potatoes go further. .Or after the potatoes are fried, just lay cheese on the top and put your lid back on and let it melt. I have a collection of cast iron skillets and bake ware and that is all I use to cook with. .Except when I make Jim's fried eggs, I use a Teflon skillet that I use only for eggs. .Jim uses my egg skillet to make popcorn in it. .Mama ain't so happy about that. .But boy he makes the best popcorn. . . But ya know, lately I told the Lord. ."What more could I give my readers than a picture of a homemaker in today's world." Last night as I wrote my prayers I said, "Oh Lord, help me to be the best homemaker of all. .Help me not to just make soap once in a while, but to make it all the time ..To show a pattern of good works." Not that I don't have the money to buy soap, as I do. .But I don't want to use my liberty to cause another woman to sin. .I want to be an example. .

Now that I have the attention of some of you, I want to show you a true working mother. .a mother in the home. .I know how to do that .."But Lord please keep me steady and diligent in the things of God." ..Every day, I think of the mothers with children who roam the streets of NYC.. My kids tell me about them.. "Mom whole families are out walking around with their children." It breaks my heart!!! I think, "Man this doesn't have to be." ...A woman of faith would know what to do. .And I don't say that casually. I have been there. .When I first moved here in 1973, there were these huge water bugs that lived in the root cellar. .They were hard to get rid of, but I got rid of them. .I never see a bug in this house now. .I mean an occasional fly or some ants but they ain't hard to get rid of. .But I used boric acid all over my house and I rarely see a bug. .But I have told you many times that this house was no palace when I moved into it, while pregnant with our son. .and Jim was here a while before he was saved. .He got saved in 1979. But ya know, if a woman has a roof over her head and a stove to cook on, and running water, and a place to bed down her children and keep them warm and dry ..Then she can make a home out of anything. .

Why let someone kick you out of your home? I mean some folks would rather live on the street than in a cheap apt. .And that is just plain foolishness. .In the old days, a man would buy a piece of land he thought he could work and make a living on. .. He barely looked at the house. .Mother was to make a home out of whatever she got. .A fancy house was never a top priority. .I mean what are we doing here that we think we have to have a fancy house to care for our families? So many are poor. .We have a new class of folks in our country called the working poor. .It used to be, in our country, that you were poor if you didn't work. .Now we have families who work but are poor. .But ya know, the mother is so needed in the home, to make a place of refuge for her family. Folks' souls are needing to be fed and nourished. .Yet Mother can do things like the mothers did in the Depression era. .She can make a garden and can all of her food like the old time mothers did. They survived. So can we. .Find a cheap house to rent and fix it up yourself. .I am sure the landlord would love ya for it. .Make sure you have some space for a garden.

Jim and I were riding down main street here in our town the other day.. And right at a side yard, a mother had made a clothes- line. .She just took a rope and tied it between 2 small trees. .I said to myself, "Oh Lord bless that lil' Mother for her ingenuity." She did what she had to do to make a clothes line. . Well heck, I have had to do stuff like that. .Makin' do. . that is what it's all about. .The problem is that many mothers don't have the guts to live poor? They would rather be at a homeless shelter. .But the wise woman builds a home.

77

Keepin' House (Part 3)

And ya know, I think it is just all about not giving up. .Just trusting in the Lord to help ya to make a place, a home, for the family. .Ya know, years ago I used to go to an Amish store. . well we still go. .But I wanted to buy all the pkgs. of dried herbs, etc. .Well all I could afford was my bread flour and basic necessities...like corn oil and oatmeal in bulk. .And I would wish to have some flavored coffees and teas but heck, I had 6 children and I had to be sensible and buy what I needed, not what I wanted. .So I prayed and the Lord taught me to grow my own herbs in my yard. .He taught me to dry flowers and to make the flavored vinegars and oils. .I learned to make soap and to make all the stuff I wanted to buy. .

Often, when I would go to an Amish store, I wanted to cry. . When I would walk in, I would see all the stuff the Amish mothers put together to sell. .The works of their hands would bring a holy conviction of God upon me. .I would get so ashamed of myself, that my hands were idle and that I had no excuse for not growing my own food and herbs, for cooking and for healing. .I thought, "Lord, why don't I make my own medicine cabinet out of healing herbs?"

Ya know, back in the old days even the mothers who didn't have a garden usually made pickles in the summer and jams and jellies and ketchup. .They would buy a bushel of cukes from a farmer and some fruit to make jams and jellies. .When fall came, they would buy some bushels of apples and potatoes to keep in the root cellar for the fall and winter. Mother made bread several times a week and biscuits in between. Mother did what she could to make a home. Each day she looked over the home and decided, "Now what do I need to buy at the store, and what can I make with my hands." Or, "How much money can I save on the grocery bill so that I can give my husband some money back to pay bills with?" Oh how I would scrimp and save in August to give Jim money back out of the groceries to be able to pay our taxes in the fall. .That was my job to make food for the table and to do it wisely. .it was my burden too.. to pay the taxes. .I stayed hidden away unto God and listened to His voice.

My family needed me at home. .And even now Jim would be lost if I went out and got a job. .He loves coming home to home cooked meals and to a wife who loves him and puts his dignity first. .Yesterday, early in the morning, Jim took me to the Amish village .He gave me a roll of bills to buy stuff with ..But I wanted to honor the Lord and still buy supplies to make things with. I bought Baby Rose some darling cloth hankies for 39 cents apiece. .Grand daddy bought her a book for children on prayer and a color book.. I got her another color book and a book about the Three Kittens. ..I needed thread and some other sewing supplies too. .Yes Mothers, no matter what, "make a home." Our country is not so poor in the physical as they are in the soul. .Folks run about with no answers for their ache in the heart.. They have a gnaw in their stomach that they can't name. They need a home ..a rest for their souls. .A place to be loved and honored as a special family member. .A place where Mother is there fussing over them and telling them to clean up their plate and to drink their milk. .To wash their hands and faces when they get up in the morning. .

My deepest prayer today is, "Oh Lord make me an example of a keeper at home ..For my own daughters and sons, and daughters- in- law. .And make me to be an example through my writings to others."

The Letters

{Part II}

- Entering Widowhood-

78

Household Duties

Dear Kitchen Saints, Good Morning!! We will get to have
Baby Rose today and we are happy about that. . David and Tiff
take care of an apt. complex. . David does most of the work but
Tiff needs to help clean today. . Tiff has become a stay- at-
home mother. . I am so happy about this. . We still help out
with Baby Rose about once a week. . David is learning to repair
the appliances at the apts. and does remodeling etc. So the
kids are doing good. . Tiff does paperwork and has an office at
home. . But she can care for Baby and does a good job. .
Anyway I am making chili for the day. . It's only 6:30 and I am
making soup. . I don't make it hot, and Baby will eat it too. .
Also I have made some fresh yogurt and it's nice and thick. .
Jim will buy some fresh fruit and we will have the yogurt. .

My favorite would be a can of stewed peaches with bananas
and the yogurt on the top. . I think if I could give you one
household tip that has helped me a lot through the years, it
would be. . to get up early in the morning and start a meal for
the day . . I used to always do that when all the children were
home. . This way if your day gets busy, then you always have a

meal ready and you don't have to think about it. . And often on a Saturday, if we had to do errands, we most always took the kids with us . . Well of course they are hungry right when ya get home at noon. . And I think often if we have a meal on the stove, then the family doesn't resort to junk food or fast food . . One quick meal I used to make for the family that is simple is just Sloppy Joes. . I would just fry up a pound of hamburger, and drain it and put in a can of tomato soup. . My kids liked it just plain like that . . Or you could add mustard onions, green pepper and spices. . Also for another meal I would just fry hamburger and drain it . . I would cook it in my big cast iron Dutch oven with the bale handle. . Then I would add vegetables. . whatever I had. . And over the top, I would pour a can of tomato soup, or any soup I had. . I would dilute it with water . . . about 3 cans of water. . Then just put this back in the oven and let it bake on low. . This way if you have to go to the store or whatever then you have a nice comfort food to come back home to. .

My grown children miss these soups and stews and often talk about them. . Dan says he doesn't like for me to make soup in the crock pot as he is used to the big black pot on the stove. . Cast iron does give food a different flavor. . I like it too. . And then I always had homemade bread to eat our meals with. . If it wasn't a yeast bread, I would make baking powder biscuits, cornbread or a quick bread. . Peanut Butter Bread was good. . I haven't made that in a long time..The quick breads are easy to make . . I loved them as I didn't get out my mixer for these as you just stir them up like you would muffins. . . I enjoy stirring things up in my bowl with a favorite spoon. . I have a nice collection of crock bowls and also I collect the speckled enamel spoons. . I have all sizes and I have the blues, blacks, and reds..This is what I enjoy looking for at Garage Sales in the warmer months..I don't like to get an electric mixer out when the family is all home as you can't hear anything when it is on. . . Also you can't cook and mix things up and talk at the same time. . I like to visit and teach my daughters and daughter- in-laws what I am doing as I cook. . And they give me some modern tips too which I love. .

One of my favorite kitchen chores is when Papa and me are here alone in the evening. . And I will stand in the kitchen by myself and stir gravy . . If it's quiet in the house, I love to stir gravy on the stove. . But if the house is busy and I have to run back and forth, I don't enjoy the stirring. . it's too hectic. . With gravy you have to stand there and stir and if ya don't it will get lumpy . . After I fry meat, I just add about a forth cup of flour to the skillet. . I smash it in with my spoon. . Then I add about 3 cups of milk, or water, and stir.

79

Our Family

Dear Sisters of Wisdom, . . Good Morning....I have so much to be thankful for . . Well we all do . . Yesterday after John and Christine and lil' Romeo, age 3, came for dinner. . Oh we had fun. . Christine has been reading our newsletter and she loves it . . So we were laughing about that. . She knows Jim so some of the things I write about Jim are extra funny to her. . Then she is married to John and so she can relate to all the things I write about him. . One year Christine got John firecrackers for Christmas. . enough to last him the whole year? John took them all and taped them together with duct tape and blew them all up together. . Wow Christine was Mad! She had spent a lot of time picking out all of these neat Firecrackers and in an instant they were gone. . Also last night John was talking about when he had run all over the country at 17. . He was walking across Golden Gate Bridge in California? And called us on the suicide phone on the bridge . . Believe me, John wasn't going to commit suicide but thought it would be fun to call home on the phone, over an ocean. .

Anyway, we all laughed and had a fun time last night . . Jim got the VCR tape, "Herbie Goes Bananas." Jim watched it with Romeo in the living room . . John and Christine and I mostly visited . . Romeo loves that show. . well so does Grandpa . . I fixed spaghetti for dinner and we had a big fresh salad. . It was really good.. Then Christine and I had a bowl of peaches with the fresh yogurt I had made. . I haven't made bread lately. I hope maybe I can today. . After the kids left here, they were going to our library up town. . Christine wanted John to help her to get to the "Happy Housewifery" website on the library computer. . Their home computer broke so they hope to get a new one . . someday? But Christine seems to love my writing and is such a cheerleader for me. . Bless her heart she is a precious wife and mother. . Both John and Christine can hardly wait to have another baby. . They are both so full of fun. . . This house just rocks with JOY when John's family comes to visit. . John is really easy goin' and funny. . Christine is more of a firecracker personality. . that's why we all love her. . David and Tiff and John and Christine just sorta laugh and joke as they go. . Both couples are bubbly and witty. . they love to tell funny stories. . David and Tiff take care of these apts. where they live. . So they have plenty of funny stories to tell about the tenants . . The apts. are new and nice and the kids do a good job with taking care of them. . But tenants want David and Tiff to referee fights between their little children, and you can imagine the crazy things people come up with. . David and Tiff always have a funny story to tell. .

When the grandchildren get together, Romeo and Baby Rose, oh they do all kinds of things. . They are like watching the old Little Rascals Shows. . At 2 and 3 years old they are very smart. . Baby Rose calls Jim "Grandpa Jim." Monday when she came to visit she says "Grandma, you be Grandpa Jim and I will be Connie." At the grocery store, if Jim goes to another aisle, she will yell out for "Grandpa Jim". . We always get a grocery cart with the car at the bottom so she can drive the cart. . Oh I am so happy to push that thing around the store. I will say to Jim, when I know Baby is listening. ."Look Grandpa, at how fast that child can drive this car!!" And Baby will start turning both of the steering wheels as fast as she can go. . to get more attention. . I can just get lost and taken up in a cloud of Joy when my grandbabies are around me. . Baby Rose, as she enters our house, will say, "This is my house too," because I always have her toys out and I never put them away. . . I have her lil' kitchen set in my living room and this is where it has been for a few weeks. I will leave it there until this summer. . I don't want my house to look like children haven't been here.

80

On With the Show

My house is loaded with children's books . . Jim and I like to collect nice books for Romeo about cars and the big trucks . . Both of the grandchildren enjoy books. . I have Crayolas out and coloring books where they can get to them. . I let them play the piano until the men get tired of it and make them stop. . The noise doesn't bother me. . Being a writer, I have books and papers everywhere. . So I have to quick stack them out of sight when the children come. . I have plenty of stacks of books and papers in back of the couch. . In the winter, I pull the couch forward to be close to the kerosene burner. . But in the summer, I put the couch back against the wall. . So I am always stacking and restacking papers and books. .

Baby Rose loved all of her Christmas books that we had out at Christmas. . So she still wants me to read them and sing Christmas songs. . The Mickey Mouse Christmas book is her favorite. . I keep trying to hide it away so she can get on to the next season, but she manages to find Mickey Mouse no matter where he is. . And I have taught her to say, "On with the Show" in a high pitched voice like Mickey says it? " And my neighbor, and friend, Charlotte says, "Connie that is the story of your life, "On with the Show." No matter what happens you go on with the show. . And that is what we all have to do Ladies today is "Go on with the Show.". There are dishes to wash and meals to plan for . . This month I have about 5 birthdays to think about for the family. . Life seems to stop for some of the family. . But the rest of the family needs the love and nourishment of Joy and peace. .

Our lives go in seasons and as Grandmothers we rise and fall with each of our children. . and grandbabies. . I am sad for Mary and Brandon this morning and yet I have to be happy for some of my other children who are happy right now. . To keep the show on the road . . to keep the dinner plates juggling and not break any. To hold the tigers, lions, and bears at bay with a whip. . To be a funny laughing clown with a red rubber nose . . To ride a horse .. bareback, standing up and jumping through firey hoops? All of this to maintain my seeds and to bring my children to Christ. . They are comin' . . . Oh yes the Lord gives me many victories. . Each day is a day to "Go on with the Show," To make another meal . . to pray I can make it through . . Sometimes the victory comes to me a moment only before the kids hit the door with "We're here." But the victories come. . the faith and anointing comes. . And each day is new . . Aunt Toot used to tell me, when the kids were young and always doing funny tricks and lighting firecrackers, "Connie you should take these kids and go on the road." Well I guess I did somehow do that hu? I have taken 'em with me to the world of the internet. . And they have multiplied and gone beyond the first 6. . And they have brought home mates who are just as funny as they are. . And now we can all say together . . No matter what: "On With the Show."

The Show must go on . . .no matter what, the show must go on. . Through broken hearts and hearts aflame with fear we must go on and keep doin' what we know to do. . To do what is before us, and to keep being faithful in the dark as we were in the light. For the Lord Jesus is runnin' this Dog and Pony Show and thank the Lord we know that He knows what He is doing. . I don't know what I am doing, but He does. . And He is the mighty deliverer and He has been here before and knows the end from the beginning. . And, like I always say about the rapture. . I don't know if it will come before or after the Great Tribulation, but all I know is I am going with Him no matter when He goes. . When I hear Him come, I am getting my stuff ready and I am going with Him. . It's His show and His anointing . . He is the author and finisher of my faith . . Not my will but Thine. . So Sisters of Wisdom get your best dresses on, and a pretty apron, and lets, "Go on with the Show."

81

Walk By Faith (Part 1)

Dear Mothers, Good Morning. I am up makin' coffee and doing a bit of housework. Yesterday we went to Wal-Mart and wow they have some really cute plastic tablecloths. . And with placemats to match. The tablecloths are just 4 bucks. . and the placemats that I liked were 2 for a buck. . I got the design with chickens on it and signs that said "Eggs for Sale," and various other old timey farm signs. . "Fresh Butter Sold Here."

Ya know the old time mothers used to use oil cloth on their tables . . Well the plastic tablecloths remind me of these. . But many mothers still used the cloth tablecloths and put placemats down to catch the messes. As Jim and I drove through town, Jim noticed the Gas Prices goin' up. . Everything seems to be goin' up in price. . Ya know Ken Copeland was good on TV a few days ago. . He was talkin' about how we don't live from a paycheck but from the Word of God. Boy that is right on. . I mean you have to follow the rules of the Bible and the husband has to work. . But whatever honest work he does, is good work to the Lord. . Proverbs says that there is profit in all labor.

I had a friend, Linda, who was dirt poor. . They lived on this farm and she worked like a dog. . Her husband did too but he didn't bring much of a cash flow into the house. . But we Christians worried about Linda and her family all the time. . Wondering if they were even warm at night. . But they kept on goin' and never lost their family. . They just kept on workin' at whatever they saw to do. She stayed at home and cared for the children and the home. . She lived off the land as best she could. . I will never forget rolling into her dirt driveway and seeing her clothes line. . Man that thing told it all. . It fell in the middle and nothin' was hardly holdin' it up. . And oh I needed to see that at the time. . She had such a brave heart. . I was about her age and oh I was struggling with raising my own children. . And the money was never there for me when I needed it. . Anyway Linda told me that day over coffee. ."Well we sure could go on Welfare but we won't." And I thought, "Mercy these people have a lot less than the people on Welfare but they are roughin' it out with their faith.." She gave me such courage to go on. . I didn't get to see her much but always asked friends about her. . That woman was stouthearted for sure. . And we mothers had better be stouthearted too. .

Jim tells me. ."Now Connie if I get sick or anything don't call an ambulance we can't afford that. . If I am gonna die, I want to die here." I always tell him to knock it off. . I can just see me getting time in prison for not calling an ambulance. . He gets

S.S. but told them he couldn't afford Medicare as they would take out about 80 bucks. . Well of course S.S. is not enough to live on, so he works too. What a wild cowboy!! And I get stuff in the mail tellin' me that because I hadn't worked enough in my life, that I will get not S.S. and no Medicare. . So. . Miss Charlotte and I laugh about me dyin' in the street. . She says when she gets old and we are widows that she will share her S.S with me. . I mean ya may as well laugh Darlin' . . I mean this stuff in our country about Health care is unreal. . All of my kids run around with no Health Ins. except for Jimmy and Betsy {Mary}. . Either John or Christine or David or I have an ongoing toothache that we can't afford to do anything about. .

But we live by faith and not by sight. . we have to learn to live on the Word of God that He will meet our needs according to His riches in glory. . We must walk by faith and not by sight. . . I hate writing on faith!! It's so much work. To live by faith is hard enough. . But to have to write about it is hard too. . It's kinda like not wanting to get out of bed in the morning. . It's easier to stay in a comfort zone and complain. . But we are children of faith and God is expecting some of us to live by faith. Living by faith don't mean quitting your job and hoodwinkin' sorry Christians into givin' you $$. . .

82

Walkin' By Faith (Part 2)

Ya know when Jim and I moved into this house it was awful.
. . Well we moved here thinking that we would remodel. . But
then Jim and I separated. . I was 7 months pregnant. . So I
wasn't gonna get a lot done. . And when I brought my baby
home from the hospital I had no help. . And the furnace went
off in the coldest day of the year. . And the electricity kept
going off. . There were days I prayed to die. . But faith was the
victory that overcame my world. .

On the cross, Jesus broke the laws of sin and death. . We as
believers don't have to go by the laws of sin and death. . Not in
this life or in the life to come. . We don't have to have common
sense and react to the troubles going on around us. . We are to
react to the Spirit of God. . If God says in His word that He has
supplied all of our needs according to His riches in glory, then
He has. . So we bank on His word as being the truth. . More
the truth than the laws of the natural flesh and blood stuff

around us. . So here I am in this broken down house with a new baby and another child to care for. . Each morning as I got up, I had to face problems with the house. . The plumbing was bad too. . But the Lord's presence was with me. . and He said, "Connie walk by faith and see this house remodeled . .Clean and cook and go on as if the house is remodeled." So my faith job was to get up each morning and see my house remodeled. . To go on about my business, sending my son to school, and caring for my baby, and vacuuming and doing the dishes. . I had bought a house. . I had nothing, but I had bought a house and now it was up to me to inhabit it with courage. . Oh I didn't want to . . . I wanted to lay on the couch and cry. . But I had to get up and go about my Father's business. . I had to prove the Word of God in my life. . And I fought the good fight of faith and didn't give up. . And in the first year, my house I had paid 150 bucks down on, turned a profit and was worth twice as much money after I had lived there a year.

But see faith is a fight. . We have to fight the good fight of faith with all the spiritual muscles we have. . And sometimes we scare the relatives and neighbors with our fight. . Well don't get around the relatives and neighbors that bring your faith down. . . Anyway, I had to get up each morning when I was pregnant and look at the torn wall paper that hung in strips. I just ripped it the rest of the way off and went on. I began to "see" the house as remodeled and lookin' nice. . And this took the fear out of me. . Because ya see the fear is what will take ya down and make you come against your own faith. .

Fear is your enemy and it is powerful like faith. . Fear is the opposing force from Satan. . But see you have to stay in your faith and in the word of God. . The stuff in the physical that is going on around you is the truth. . it is a truth!! But the Word of God is a truth that can own the truth of the physical things going on. . See everything around you on this earth is subject to change. . But the sure Word of God is never going to change. . . He is the same yesterday, today and forever. . He, and His Word, is the ultimate truth. . We can have miracles on earth as they are in Heaven.

83

The Imperfect Mother (Part 1)

Dear Mothers, Good Morning. . Don't you love the writings describing Suzanna Wesley? Doesn't that give ya courage to go on? Suzanna's husband was in debtors prison a lot of the time. He wasn't a bad man, but he just couldn't pay his debts. So Suzanna was left at home alone much of the time to care for the children. . She had 19 children and 10 of them died. . I can't imagine losing 10 children. . I think Suzanna herself was like the 24th child of her mother's. . Imagine if her Mother had been on birth control. We would have never known Suzanna. . But through her mother's obedience and Suzanna's to God, she helped bring revival to England. . Just by staying home and teaching her children. Charles wrote many of the old songs we still sing in our churches today. . Then John was the preacher who brought revival. . Suzanna was methodical in her teachings and helped start the Methodist church. . But wow she must have had a good sound idea of what heaven was like in order to lose 10 children and still be able to get up in the morning. . That Suzanna was made out of more than flesh and blood and skin and bones. . She had to be living on the breath of God. . Actually she didn't know about Salvation through the blood when she was raising her family. . She knew the laws of the Bible. . But then later on, her son John saw in the word of God about salvation through the blood and she herself became saved too. . But even when she knew only the laws of God, she was faithful to teach her children the truth she had. .

I feel like this speaks to me. . Because I did my best to raise my children for Jesus. . With the truth I had. . and always being a day late and a dollar short. . Always on the skid like a street rat at times B.S.in my way through when my moxie was long gone. . .not to mention my faith. . .But God knows my heart that all I want out of this life is to see my children all love Jesus and to live happy lives with their families. . And no I don't know everything like Suzanna didn't either. . But she learned as she went. . . And through her faithfulness to God to do what she knew to do, she made a difference in her world for His kingdom. . All we mothers are given is a day at a time. . Each day we have to do what we know to do. We are human and married. . Ya know the Bible says that a married woman cares for the things of the world and how she may please her husband. . I was never as spiritual as some of my Christian sisters. . I see things in my heart and can sense angels about me . . But I have never seen angels in the physical. . with my physical eyes. . But ya know some of we women almost live 2 lives. . Like one of a married woman and one of a single woman who is given to prayer and spiritual things. . I lived sort of like that for the first 12 years of my marriage. . I was a married woman but had no husband. . But I gave myself to prayer and was used by God to win souls to Christ. . I never ran around with men. . I wouldn't have done that. . When Jim left me then I submitted to him and ministered to others. . But I played the part of a single woman who could give herself to prayer and witnessing. . And when Jim came home, I abandoned this ministry to live only for Jim and my children. . It is hard to flip back and forth like that and I made many mistakes. . But like Suzanna, I learned as I went. . And I pray the Lord will show me His mercy where I have made mistakes. . . But we all make mistakes on this road to holiness. .

And this is what keeps us hallow and heartsick to dwell in His presence.   His anointing can only come as we cry out with an empty heart for His Words. . Some of us who have known Him for a long time live only from one touch of His hand to the next touch. . We run from one anointing to the next one. . And some of us are a gentle mix between that single set apart woman or widow who has given herself only to God, and the married woman who has given herself only to her home.

84

The Imperfect Wife (Part 2)

And oh mercy!! Ya know we as Sisters of Wisdom want to get all of our rules and regulations set up and tacked down and then we go on. . I stand here today able to write because my friend Mary L prayed for me yesterday. . Married and divorced and remarried. . She doesn't recommend it and I don't either. . But having said that, I think some of these divorced and remarried women long so for a marriage and home that they have something to teach some of us who have never been divorced. . I AM THE IMPERFECT WIFE. I feel like I have been divorced and remarried at times because of what I went through. . So at times I can somehow let down my net and draw up the divorced wife and the married wife in the same haul. . Having been there and done that, I guess. .

Of course Jim is my first and only husband and I wouldn't recommend divorcing your mate. . But Jim and I were separated many times. . And then Jim got saved and we have been happily united now for 26 years. . None of my number of years ever add up. . Because we will have been married for40 years at the end of this year. But we had the first few years of marriage that was somewhat peaceful . .Then we had 12 yrs of separations. . So I have become a gentle mix of 2 women. . I know what it is to be abased and how to abound. . Jim now is the sweetest, most dearest man I know. . His love for me and the children is so precious. . Jim gives me a peace and a joy. . He never pushes me to do more than I can do. . I am a dreamer and writer. . I need lots of time to pray and be alone with the Lord. . And Jim understands this. . And yet I wouldn't ever think of not cooking for him and doing his laundry . . Or being here for him to come home to with the coffee hot and a meal on the stove. .

Jim loves the babies that came from my womb. . My grandbabies are precious to him. .We have invested many years of blood sweat and tears into our marriage. . When I lay beside my man at night, I know what is in his heart . .When tragic things hit our home, I know what is in his heart and he knows what is in mine. . And we work it out in silence mainly. . We don't want to confess a negative confession over our brood . . We plan on God delivering our children and making them whole and sound and in love with God. . Some of our kids are there and some are on their way there. . But none will be lost to Satan. . Not because Jim and I know what the heck we are doin'. . But we love each other. . We love our offspring. . And we want to do right. . And what else is there? We go from where we live, and we do what we can to make things honest and right with our children and our world. . And as I go along, I think of Suzanna Wesley and her life. . It wasn't all perfect, but God used her for His glory. . I don't think that any of her daughters were happily married. . But out of her 19 children she lost 10 and I think then she had like 7 daughters and 2 sons left . . I had a book on John Wesley but it didn't tell a whole lot about his mother. . I am just writing from what I remember reading about her in other books.

85

The Fat Cats (Part 1)

Dear Mothers, Good Morning. . I am up makin' coffee and straightening up the house. . it is so cold in this house. . and my e-machine gets cold. . So the keys stick and have to be warmed up. . So I do some replies to get the keys warmed up and then I do the regular writing. .We put our heat down to just over 60 degrees at night. . So when I come out here it is COLD. . I have to get warm and my e-machine too.

Sunday I needed to rest so watched this telethon for this Christian channel. . Funny? Oh my mercy!!! Well this one Fat cat was kinda interesting at first . . Not scriptural by any means but he was good for entertainment. . I just wanted to be distracted for a while. . So he tells everyone how he gave his money away until he became rich. . Well you know he is tryin' to hoodwink the sheep into givin' him their money. . The funny part is he acts like his audience is money-starved-monkeys. . And if it does indeed work, to give money, and you get all this money back, then why doesn't he give more money so he can get more back? And why is he buggin' the sheep for money? If it's that easy, what's he doin' on TV beggin'? And ya know money is not what most people need to make it. . When I get down-and-out you could throw 20 dollar bills at me all day long and it wouldn't help me. . If I don't hear from God and if He doesn't help me, then no amount of money will help. . I mean some of us do need money but we need a word from the Lord first. . If we can get a word from the Lord, then the money will come. But to run out and chase money is the wrong way to go. . And sure we need an open hand to give and to receive. . But this plan of give your money away to the hungry wolf and expect it to return so you can pay the rent. . No!! . . . And this was a message that started in the 70's and if it had worked, all of us Christians would be millionaires by now. . But all it did, in reality, was to make the Fat Cats Fatter? So now they are doing good, and the believers are getting' poorer. . . See the wolves try to get you to think that the more money you have, the more blessed you are. . But the word says that some among us suppose that gain is godliness and from such we need to turn away. . Jesus was poor and lowly of heart and He is our example. .

Often when I hear the Cats cry out for their money, I think of Mother Theresa in India. Oh what an example she has been to me. . She was a true servant of God . . Who but a true servant like her would drag dying unbelievers out of the sewer to wash them of maggots and tell them of the love of God.

Those Cats on TV wouldn't dirty their hands to do that. . They want your money and that is all they want. .

See this teaching starts out with telling the Christians they should have the best house and the best car and the nicest clothes, and on and on. . So the Cats tell the wife this too, as often she is there at church without her husband. . So the lil' woman thinks she needs a better job so she can be blessed by God better and be able to give Hungry Fat Cat more money $$. . . So the preacher has Mother out workin' her buns off at an outside job so that she can be blessed. . It's a teaching that makes women slaves and they can never relax and be a mother and keeper at home. . .

Sure Fat Cat gets more money all the time and he is indeed rich. . Ya know why? Because you are driven by the sins of your own lusts and pride and you keep given him money. . And he keeps goin' with his message because he makes a lot of money at it. . But it ain't all about money. . And why not work for your money the old fashioned way? It's a lot easier and more honest. . See folks are payin' for a lifestyle and not a life. . Many are so in debt and will die that way.

86

The Fat Cats (Part 2)

See it's not a sin to be poor. . Jesus made no reputation for Himself and we shouldn't either. . He was man enough to be poor and honorable and we should be too. . All of this debt that some folks live under just so they can look good is ridiculous. . I barely spend any money because there is little I want. . I am happy that I hung onto our home through many trials and now it is paid off. . I have something to leave my children so each of our 6 children will have some money to put down on a house. We want to leave something behind for our kids. . . And how many times before we remodeled did friends tell me I should move and get a fancy apartment? Well I could squander my children's inheritance, but I think that would be an ungodly thing to do. . And to be poor with dignity and purpose is a rare life these days. . But who has enough guts to do that? It takes some strength of character. . Who are you if you have nothing but yourself to offer. . I mean without the expensive car?

I came from a background of upper middle class. . As a child, I had everything. .The best of clothes, etc. . Dad had a good factory job and always a nice car, boat, and we went on nice summer vacations etc. . But my life was empty and void to me. . I needed Jesus and when I met Him, I got rich. . . I call Jim my Million Dollar Baby. . I mean when he was down-and-out, no amount of money could set him free. . But Jesus, my Daddy, heard my cry and He gave Jim deliverance. . My rich Daddy, Jesus, loved me so much and heard my cries for a husband to love me and gently care for me as a Good Shepherd here on earth. . Jesus knew that I wanted to have children for His glory. . Jesus heard my cries and gave me a husband to love me and care, and to shelter me . . I had no money when Jim got healed. . I gave Jesus my life . . not my money. . Jesus can't be paid off like a Mafia gangster. . so that you can get your needs met? To pay Fat Cat for protection? I mean we are children of the Most High God. . He is spiritual and we must worship Him in Spirit and in Truth. He asks His followers for no more than He, Himself, gave . . His life!! He wants our life rich or poor. .

And Fat Cat says he wants the money for the Gospel's sake. . And I have never heard some of them preach the gospel. . All they preach on is how to give them your money. . And they ain't gonna preach anything else no matter how much money you throw at them. . Same way with Public Education. Folks think we need to throw out more money for better teachers. . And then our kids will be able to read. . No . . what we need is the truth and this sets the captive free. . One man with the truth will go anywhere in the world without money. . I can give my message out for free to anyone . . And if I get so full of truth that I outgrow my e-machine? Then God could take me anywhere He wanted me to go. Sarah never had any money or Mary, Jesus' Mother. Their lives were so faithful that God Himself published them. . God shares His glory with no man. . And certainly the gospel won't be preached according to the money we give away. . And the best preachers are the ones who will preach to ya and worry if you have enough money for your own family. . .Remember Reverend Alden in "Little House on the Prairie?" He cared for his sheep and was poor for their sakes. . And this is how all the old time preachers were. . And they were always like that in our country up until about the 70's when they got ahold of this idea of seed money etc. . But before that the Christian families gave what they could and preacher was expected to live on that. He, and his family, was often poor but that made him a good preacher. . He suffered with the struggling families in his congregation. .

I will never forget Pastor Hawkins . . He was Jim and my first Shepherd. .He was just out of Dallas Seminary and boy did God use Jim and me to break this young preacher in. . But he went for the ride and hung on for dear life. . God Bless him.

87

All is Well [3/21/ 2006]

[On 3/18/ 2006, Jim was admitted into the hospital with a heart attack. He had triple by-pass surgery.]

Dear Mothers, I am up making coffee this morning. . I have to get dressed and get ready to go to the hospital to see Jim. . My neighbor, Miss Charlotte, takes her lil' granddaughter to school in the morning, so I will ride with her as she goes past the hospital. Jim is progressing. I hope they can take the breathing tube out of his mouth today. . Then he should be getting out of the intensive care unit. . Christian Joy called last night crying as she thought she had more money that she did. . So won't be able to come to Iowa until the first part of April. . I told her that was a good time anyway as I didn't want the kids to all come at once and then all be gone. My children are such a comfort to me. .

All of my children have cried and cried. Jimmy didn't as he is more stoic. . .But my children, for the most part, are so expressive and have just bawled over Daddy. . And the last conscious words he said to the kids through the oxygen mask was, "You boys take care of your Mother." Jim is a champion

of a man and will be strong for all of us. . Our Mary is like a lil'
child for me to hold. . I heard her crying down the hall as she
had just heard about Jim and came running to me crying
"Mama." Oh those kids!!

One funny story before I go. . Sunday night, as Jimmy
brought me home from the hospital, he stood in the doorway
both feet planted firmly on the ground as he said, "Well Mom I
would like to get upset about all of this but I know you
wouldn't have it. . The whole time we were growin' up, you
wouldn't make a big deal of sickness. . If Johnny had chopped
his arm off, you would have said, 'Oh it's ok . . it will be
alright.' So I guess you will be ok now." I laughed and said,
"Yes Jimmy it will be alright." . . Well I gotta rock and roll and
get dressed, as I just have an hour to get ready. . . And yes, all
is well.

88

Old Time Mothers

Ya know how I told you the story about Jimmy, our son who drove me home from the hospital Sunday night? How he said, "Mom I would like to get real upset over this but I know you won't have it?" . . Well there was a 2nd part to this story too. . I told Jimmy, "Ya know Honey the old time Mothers were like that. . they were strong. . . A mother who had children stayed calm as to not upset all of her family.". . I mean you want to keep the faith goin' and not let sorrow and fear take over. . I told Jimmy, "Ya know Gram {my mother} just cheered us all on when Grandpa {my dad } died. . The Mother plays a very important role in the healing of the family. . She has to hold them strong . . . It won't do for the mother to fall apart . . She is older and should have a handle on her faith. . The young adult children don't have the experience in faith to hold on when things go wrong." And we Mothers teach our children valuable lessons as we stand strong when the winds of adversity blow. . We can tell our kids, "You need God," But they are not impressed with that. . Many times a mother must walk alone through the valley of the shadows to show her kids how to do it. . Very valuable lessons are taught and cut into our children's souls as we don't fall when Satan pushes us . . Oh I am flesh and blood and so human. . So full of fear at times. . But if I was a naturally strong person, then God couldn't use me. . I have to be able to be easily touched by my children and my dear husband. . We want to be hard sometimes so that we can't be hurt. . But God uses we mothers in our tenderness. . We are married women and are helpers and not lady preachers. . We are to get under our families and undergird them with our faith and love.   Not our perfectness . . so perfect that we can't be touched. .We are made from our men . . . their helpers. . . We should be strong to talk to the Drs and to let them know that we are capable of making it all the way through.

Miss Charlotte was such an encouragement to me in all of this. . I wore a nice long winter coat to the hospital. "Connie you look rich. Your coat matches your eyes." I knew that she was tryin' to add her strength to mine. . She knew I was worried about how we would pay for all this luxury. . By the way, I got the coat at the Salvation Army for 2 bucks. . But it is a "London Fog" and is all wool and full length . . But ya know we have to be women of strength and dignity. . I wanted the Drs and nurses to know that Jim had family that loved and adored him. . And that we wanted the best of care for him. . I told his nurse, "Jim is much loved of his children and grand children. . He is a wonderful husband to me. We have been married almost 40 years." I was covering the fear that was in my heart and I really wanted to say, "Please don't make any mistakes with Jim's life. I would die without him." But of course we are women of dignity right? And we only open our mouth with wisdom; and kindness is the law upon our lips. Well I need to get goin' and see what needs to be done for the day. . We, as the Hultquist Family, appreciate your prayers for our dear Jim. . He is much better but still in Intensive Care.

89

Living on Love (Part 1)

Dear Mothers, Good Morning. . Well I will be off to the hospital here this morning. . Jim had a few irregular heartbeats and so he will be in the hospital a few more days. . We were hoping that he could have come home today. . Boy he has been antsy, and me too. . I pray he had a good sleep last night. . . I am having good and bad days, and so is Jim. . But I guess that is the way it goes. . I am just glad that Jim is alive. Oh man I would've hated to lose him. . Still he says he has no pain in his chest or leg where they took out the veins for his heart. . .He did say he had a headache the other night. . I know, if I had open heart surgery I may get a headache. . Jim has been so antsy and that has worried me. . The kids are very supportive and have been in and out each day. . Bless their hearts that have been so worried. . Jim seems a bit loopy. . but I guess that is par for the course. . Some men are not good patients. . He is good for the nurses and all but he just hates being at the hospital. . He longs to get home and I long to get him home. Just pray that his heart will beat steady. . .

Our children have been so precious. . Some of them have given us money and some are waiting for when they can . . But Jim has always been generous with them and now they have come up to the bat for us. . I guess we live by faith hu? I took my Bible to bed with me last night. . I read Proverbs and about wisdom. . This gives me peace. . Lately I keep seeking the Lord's heart. . I mean with all the crazy preachin' goin on ya think, "what is the answer?" And I think 'Well God's ways are so above our ways" I think "How can we know Him?" And yet we are made in His image. . We are made like Him. . I think He wants to be a part of us and wants to fellowship with us. . He works with our desires as we follow Him. .

Just like how He picked Sarah to have a supernatural birth when she was old. . Sarah had longed for children all of her life. . God didn't pick a woman who never wanted children to begin with. . Sarah was missing the mark in the beginning because she wasn't submissive and she jumped ahead of God by giving Abe her servant girl to have a child by. . Sarah wasn't perfect but God dealt with her and showed her where she had to change in order to see her prayers answered. . He saw something in Sarah that He could use. . And most of what He used was her burning desire to have a child. . God uses our desires if our desires are based in Him. . I want Jim to be healed and be able to come home. . God will use my prayers as I long for my husband and long to please him. . The Bible says that we have an unction from the Holy Spirit and we know all things. . So if we chase God and long for Him, then we know all things. . As we long after Him, then this is our path of righteousness. .

God used Esther to save her people. . She had a love for her own family and her relatives. . She was passionate about saving her people. . And she laid her life on the line because of her love for her family. . Had she been a lesser woman, who cared only for pleasure for a season, she would have thought, "Well what can I do about all of this. I can't save anyone, I would be killed.". . But no she was a virtuous woman and strength and honor were her clothing. . She remained honorable and strong even though she had the bad news that all of her relatives were about to be murdered. . I don't think she even understood what she did really. . I think she just remembered her own relatives . . the ones she was close with. . She didn't want to see them die. . I don't think she was all that religious about it. . But out of her own heart, she didn't want to see her loved ones die. . Of course she saved the Jewish nation and she saved the lineage of Christ. . But I doubt she realized that at first. . Esther was just doing what Esther was used to doing. She obeyed her uncle as she always had as a child. . And in so doing she did something revolutionary. . She also understood the authority of the King . .

90

Esther or Vashti (Part 2)

And ya know Esther understood that her husband, the King, wasn't even a believer. . But she knew that he was her authority. . She pleased the king with her meekness and her beauty. . The King loved Esther and she pleased him. . She obtained grace and favor. . The King saw that he could give his heart to her. ."The heart of her husband safely trusts in her." . . Oh God, please give we ladies today the heart of Esther. . She obeyed God in the face of fear. . Esther obeyed her uncle in her childhood home. . She had a habit of obeying the head of the house. . And as she continued to do this, she saved a nation. That is so powerful. . .

And oh my silly kids!! Dan has a new tattoo that says, "Lord save my soul." I said to Dan, "I hope the Lord does save your soul. " And he said, "I do too.". . On John's time sheet at work, it says John and then his number is 316. . So Christine says, every time she sees it, she sees John 3:16. . The Lord has such a heavy calling on my children. . Like a holy mist of oil about them. . Mother's tears and prayers surround them. I love their Daddy and I love them and the grandbabies. . They are far from perfect for sure. . But they were brought up to respect their parents and they sure have been there for us. . Dan gave us 95 bucks and told us he didn't need it. . All of the kids have been so sweet. . Oh what stinkers, but they are obeying God as they respect Jim and I. . They are so glad Papa didn't die. . And they have to know it was a miracle. . They were all there when the Dr. said it was a good chance that he would die in surgery. . Yesterday, as Jim's brother was at the hospital, he asked Mary and Brandon if they knew Jesus and they both said they did. Bob asked Mary, "Do you read the Bible Mary?" And she said, "Oh yes I read about 4 translations." And I know she does. . But those kids can get into more trouble. . I guess it all has to do with their calling. But for me as their mother. . mercy what a life. . But I know I love God and I want to do His will. . I have a passion to know Him and to walk with Him. . I don't want to sin or give my life to this world. . And so as I go, I have to know that He is with me. . I don't sin on purpose and I know that He is with me to forgive me. . Sometimes our lives go terribly wrong. .

I imagine that Daniel thought of that when he got thrown in the lion's den. . He had obeyed God and was thrown in a den to be eaten. . I imagine he may have thought, "Hey thanks a lot." But, no, Daniel prayed and God saved him. . And just think Daniel's life was written about in the Bible. . His act of faith was published. . Daniel wasn't of this world. He lived by the rules of another world. . He was a dreamer and a visionary. He heard the voice of God. . And "as he went.". as he obeyed

God. .he saw many miracles. . it was a habit with Daniel to put God first and to obey Him even in the small things. .

And I will never forget, as a young mom, sitting rocking my baby and I prayed to Jesus. . "Lord, is this all I am called to do?" And Jesus said to the ears of my heart. ."Connie your life will be told all over the world." I thought the Lord meant all over my town. . Of course I couldn't understand that I would write about all the victories I have written about. . I didn't know the goodness of God or what the Lord would do in my life. . But I kept calling upon Him and He kept answering me and showing me great and mighty things that I knew not. . He was testing me and wanting to know what I would do. . You know? In the dark, in the tight places? What was I like when it was just me and the children at home? When Jim wasn't there, who was I? . . When no one could see me, who was I? He was watching me and the angels were with Him. . "Who is this Connie girl? . . . Will she walk with Me? . . Even when she looks stupid and all seems to be lost?" He talked it over with the angels. . Jesus wondered, "should I marry her ..and share my secrets with her?" Each of we wives' lives hang in the balances. . . Will we be an Esther or a Vashti?

91

Night Angels and Holy Winds

Dear Mothers of the Hearth, . . .Oh yesterday I could sense the angels all about me. . . Last night, as I went to bed, I could see with the eyes of my spirit. . I saw night angels blowing in holy anointed winds. . Oh these angels were running swiftly like horses full of passion . . Warring Angels . .They were running and drifting and talking with such urgency to each other. . Sometimes in the vision they reminded me of jets streaking across the night sky. . And I could see lights flashing about them. . They were saying, "We love God and we are urgent to serve Him. . . For those who will minister to the least of them, we run with passion to serve God's servants. . Those who will minister to the least are God's anointed. . And we want favor with God. . . And the way we get favor is to minister to the ones who minister to Him. . We run swiftly to look for the servants of God who pull on His heart.". . Oh, these angels were running so fast. . I don't know how fast but like jet airplanes. . And I could see flocks of them coming from all over the world, coming to me to help me. . Not because they loved me. . But because they loved God and wanted His favor. . They have such a passion to be the Lord's servants. . They watch Jesus and they long to please Him and to do His will.

And the Lord said to me, "Open up my kingdom. Pull out the gold and the silver. . All I have is yours. " And the Lord knows that I am not interested in gold and silver, and I know He is meaning spiritual gold and silver. . He means the wisdom of God . . What would I do with Money? I need a healing for Jim and one for Brandon and one for my broken heart. . So I ask the Lord to send a third of His angels to Jim, and a third to Brandon and Mary, and a third to me to soothe my heart. . And God is even now soothing me. . He says to me over and over, or as if He is speaking to my enemies. . ."Touch not mine anointed and do her no harm. ." He is Father to me . . And He is holding me close. . I can feel His warmth and love. . He pierces my heart with His love . . His sweet breath and words fall upon my face. . He promises to protect me and go with me through this valley of the shadows . .

I just called the hospital and Jim needs prayer. . His heart rate is not stable. Pray for Jim please. . Please have a prayer chain pray. . Please ask everyone to pray. . His heart has to get stable. . I can see Holy Angels coming from all parts of the world to minister to Jim. . Please pray. . we don't want to lose him. . .

92

Jim Died (Part 1)

[4/1/2006]

My husband died. . . All of the kids are here. . They are sleeping here tonight. . I am up in the night brokenhearted. . .I will miss Jim so much. . Please pray for my kids as they are taking it hard.

[Later]

I can't believe he died. . I don't know what will become of the group? It seems the more I suffer, the bigger the group gets. . I would like to keep it going as cheerfully as possible. . So many suffer and need this group. . I hope we can keep it as usual. . . I am a widow now. . I can't believe I am a widow now. . My mercy how many hats do I have to wear? I am writing because it helps ease my pain. I have always written to ease my pain. I can't hardly see the screen, as I have the big light in the dining room off as the kids are all bedded down in the living room. .

As we grieved at the hospital, the Chaplin there said, "I have never seen a lovelier family. . you have so much love for each other.." I had told the kids, each one as I hugged them, Don't send flowers to honor your Dad. . Love each other as brothers and sisters. . Love your families and your children..This is how you will honor Papa". .

Dan cried out over Jim, "Oh Papa . . oh Papa. ." over and over again, he cried out for Papa. I had been up earlier with Chrissy. ."Why isn't he responding to us?" I asked, and they said he was just tired. . But I knew something was wrong. . I said to Papa. . "Are you just very tired Jim?" And he nodded yes. . I covered him for the night, and tucked him in. . A few hours later he died. . My loving family is all here with me. Brothers and sisters hugged and comforted each other. . Just as Jim would have wanted. .

I will write my way out of this . . As the devil tries me, I will write for the glory and honor of Jesus. . Satan haunts me with condemnation. . He is the accuser of the brethren. . Didn't I have enough faith? Prolly not. . Did I do some things wrong? I am sure I did. . I am flesh and blood and am never perfect. . God forgive me and keep my sorry soul. . And in this death, I want to show His glory. .

Jim's last request to the kids was, "Take care of your Mother." And they say to me over and over, "Mom don't worry we will take care of you.". . And I know they will. . Oh I guess in the back of my mind I thought maybe Jim would die but I sure never planned on being a widow now. . I wonder if I am only a writer poured out. . I always wondered how Mary lived through losing her baby. . Now I know. . one day atta time. . "One second at a time". . Oh, may His grace be sufficient for my children and me. . .May the Lord comfort the pain and grief about me. .Give me new visions, Lord . . New depths of understanding. .

93

His Grace (Part 2)

I think of the story I once read about one of the Saints of old. As the believers were being burned at the stake they said to the next one to go: "Hold up one finger if God's grace is sufficient for you as you burn." And as the fire rose up the saint's feet, he held up 2 fingers instead of one to say that God's grace is more than sufficient. . I ache with pain all over with heartache as I write. . And yet one day I will understand His grace . . His grace is sufficient for us, as the Word says it is. . By faith I receive His grace and mercy. . Jesus has come to bind up the broken in heart and to set the captive free. .

I pray for His grace as I need it for today. . Jesus is Lord of all. He is the beginning and the end. . The same power that raised Christ from the dead, dwells in me and in you. . All things work together for good to those who love God and are called for His purpose. . He will walk with me through the valley of the shadows of death. . . and I fear no evil as He is with me. ."Lord make me strong as I honor my husband on this day."

94

The Hultquist Home (Part 1)

Dear Mothers, this morning I woke up singing a song that Jason {Chrissy's boyfriend} had played on the piano. . It is a song to Jesus, a very simple love song. . . I thought, "Well at least I won't be waking Papa up.". . Christian Joy heard me from the upstairs bedroom and I know I woke her. . She ran down the stairs and listened at my bedroom door . . I think she thought I was crying. . Bless her heart!!! Anyway, we played a lot of music yesterday. . Homemade music. . Dan made a ...? Well I would call it an Appalachian cello. You make it with a washtub, a broom handle, and a clothesline rope. . He made one and played it like a cello. . I played a spoon on an old washboard. . Jason played the piano and David the guitar. . We also had an old time harmonica we played. . Jason said that I played the washboard really well. Maybe he was kidding, I don't know. . .Of course it's in me ya know. . that mountain music. .

Folks came in and out all day yesterday. . We have food galore here but I never have time to set the table. . Mary Elisabeth is a flurry of plans for the Memorial. . I think the funeral website says it will be held here at our home . . But we have rented a hall for this, as our home is too small. . I will tell Mary to change it on the internet. . Many people I think are coming. . So many friends are bringing food. . So many have given money . . thanks to all who have. . We all joke that Mary should get a job as a funeral director. . She runs about with her notebook and pen making all the arrangements. . All I am good for is to sing and sit and wonder what I will do next. . Mary and I talked last night. I told her I would have to get a job. . "Oh Mom no . . what will you do? I don't want my mom to work. . You have never worked outside the home." I said that I would do housekeeping for someone or babysit . . My house was such a mess when Chrissy got here. . So Mary says to me, "Now Mom we know you can't keep house. . so don't try that you would get fired!!!" Mary says, "Mom I don't want you out cleaning someone else's house. .We kids will take care of you." But of course my kids have their own lives and I will find a way to make an income. . I want my kids to have a fighting chance to care for their own families. . I want to continue to encourage them and help them if I can. . I am a bit weak now, but I will rise again. . I will get back up. .

Of course Papa, and my writings about him and his babies, will always come first. . He is my first and only husband and I will do him good for the rest of my life. . Jill came over yesterday. . Aunt Toot and Ruth. . Good friends who have been close to me for years. . They are jewels . . priceless jewels. . Lots of young people come by to pay their respects. . They knew Jim loved them and wanted good for them. . it's such a bittersweet time. . Toot says that now I will show my readers how to get through being a widow. . You get through it all honestly and with reverence towards your husband. . I sat yesterday with a blanket in Jim's chair. . I guess I could feel his comfort there.

95

All is Well (Part 2)

Well I need to get busy. . The clocks have to be turned ahead today. . All of us were exhausted yesterday. . We had cleaned the living room over and over but in the end we had to leave it alone. . The children have toys all over the house which is honey to my heart. . Still if folks come by, they would fall over the toys. . Oh the food galore has been brought in. . No one will go hungry today. . For lunch today we will have Lasagna and French bread brought in by Mary and Russ . . my mentors. . I don't know who will be here. . But I need to take a bath and get cleaned up, and clean up the house. .

Christiane Joy is still asleep. . Boy she brought her boyfriend home and he is staying here too? I hate to tell Christiane this but that guy is a Christian I think? Or one in the making. . He is a simple guy but he is like Jesus among us. . I call him my Chauffer. . He is so quiet in his manners, and our girl seems to think her Jason is what life is all about. . I told them "No sleeping together in my house." And they let me know without me asking that no funny business is goin' on. . I told Jason that if he ever hurt my girl I would come after him as that is "all" I would have to do now that Jim isn't here to hold me down. . We all laugh over that. .

Yesterday I folded laundry and put Jim's clothes in his drawer. It seems so strange that he will never wear these clothes again.   Life happens and we think our lives won't ever change but they do. . I think of the scriptures and the Virtuous woman. . The Bible says that she did her husband good all the days of HER life, not his life. . The old home place is still here and the children are all well and the grandchildren. . . All is well. . . All is well.

96

Keepin' Busy

Dear Mothers, I am up late this morning. . The kids all stayed up late as Jimmy just got here around 7 last night. . . So anyway I stayed in bed this morning. . The Memorial will be today . . this evening at 5 p.m. . . Mary Elisabeth is a flurry of ideas about Daddy's Memorial. . Tiff and Christine are all doing the Memorial too. . Christian Joy has mainly been here with me doing what needs to be done. . . Each of my precious children have played a part. . Papa is right; his babies can do no wrong. . Susie, Dan's wife, made a delicious spaghetti supper for us last night. . Then another of their friends brought in the cheesy potatoes. . It was a feast let me tell ya. . Jason, Chrissy's boyfriend, said ,"Wow I come from a small family. . I have never seen so much food go in and out of a house before. . And I have never seen so many dishes." And why I haven't used paper plates and cups I don't know. . The kids all take turns doing dishes. . Every time I start on the dishes I am interrupted. . And then some kid comes along and does the dishes. . But I have phone calls and folks at the door to tend to. . I am busy with just the happenings about me. . Baby Rose will stand with her blanket and want me to rock her. . Of course she is top priority. ."Grama, rock me in the chair." . .

Dan said that all of his friends will come to the Memorial. . I am thinking, "How nice a side show again . . But where would I be if my life was normal." Dan said that all of his Punk Rock friends loved Dad. . They got a kick out of him looking at them and then at Dan and saying, "Where did these freaks come from?" That was Jim's first take on it. . Then he would be nice and attempt to shake hands with 'em. . After he was done smoking, he would say, "Well, they will come out of it. . I wasn't so hot when I was their age.". . Papa could forgive a rattle snake if he was called to do so. . Him and I were just 2 good forgivers and that's how we remained married. . And ya know I don't regret Jim's passing. . I shudder when I think of him at the hospital. . he hated it there. . Thank God he is now with the Lord. . It killed me to see Jim with that tube down his throat. . It would have killed me to see him like that for a long time. . Each morning as I get up I think, "Papa was so tired it was his time to go. . Why didn't I see how tired he was?" And I told this to Mary and Brandon. . And really all the kids tell me, "Mom, Dad always seemed young. . We thought of him as young." Well ya know Jim's wife never wanted to give up and just be old either. . We lived our lives right up until Jim died. . He went to work and I stayed home and kept the home fires burning. . I guess that is sure a lot to be glad about. . PTL. . I will miss Papa but I am glad he is in a better place and not suffering. . So today is a day to remember. The Memorial will be at 5 and Mary is ordering the boys to be there at noon. . Mary who is always late is ordering the boys to be there at noon? Hmm !!!

Well for the entertainment, Jason will sing and our friend Glenn will play the bagpipes. . I am praying that Chuck will give a wonderful invitation to receive Christ. He always does. It wouldn't surprise me if we got some folks who will come forward. . I am praying they will. Please pray that folks will receive the Lord today. . My brother's wife Shelly is such a hoot. . She says, "Ya know Connie I never like to miss any of your functions as I get to see things I have never seen before." She gets me to laughing. . . She means all the Mohawk haircuts and faces full of piercings. . Kids who are tattooed everywhere. . . If ya want a good laugh, think of Fred in the midst of all of this. . I try not to think of it. . I am thinking of having one of my kids just sit with Fred to keep him calm. . I was thinking of Jimmy for that job. . Just pray that Fred won't kill us for being such pirates. . If he comes after me I am just gonna say, "Papa's babies can do no wrong. . . That's what Papa says."

97

Resting

The Memorial is over. . It was lovely and all the kids did such a good job. . But I almost fainted. . I was very weak. . I will write about the Memorial later on. . My children did so well and I am so proud of all of them. . I did nothing but keep my body and soul connected. . I am so glad that Jim is safe in heaven with Jesus. . And now I have to go on for the rest of my life. . What a tall order!!!

I am anxious to do my homemaking. I long to make some veggy soup with hamburger. . I just long to have the house smell and look as it always has. . Papa's spirit is here and he still comforts me. . Oh ya know? No matter what happened in my life with Jim, we somehow we went home when it was over. . We watched some TV, had some coffee and went on with the rest of our lives. . And I will do that too, only Jim is in heaven now.

98

No Regrets (Part 1)

Dear Mothers, I am up in the night for a bit. . thinking about the cards so many have sent. . Christian Joy is so good to help me with all of them and to make sure Mom don't lose any of the money in the cards. . I am so deft at doing business. . Jim took care of everything to do with paying the bills etc. Soon I will be left to my own devices. . God only knows how I will handle things. . Well I did it alone for many years and can do it again. . Just getting my mind around it all is what I need to do. I will do fine once I get at it. .

I have been so dizzy lately but when I woke up in the night just now, I feel the dizzy feeling has left. . I feel stronger. . more confident. . My greatest worry is for my children that they will worry too much over me. . I am fine and no one need worry. . I feel so sorry for my friends . . .So many are so grieved about Jim's death. . I was grieved when he suffered in the hospital, but I am not grieved now. . I know he is not suffering. I have no regrets. . Wild man and I gambled with life right up to the end. . We knew he would die something like this. . The Lord had it all in His hands. . I have no regrets. . The Lord gave me almost 26 years of Joy with Jim . . The Lord promised me double JOY for all the 12 years of heartache in the first years of my marriage. . He promised me and He gave me much Joy and happiness in the past years. . We would have been married for 40 years in the fall of this year. . 12 years and 26 years don't add up to 40. . But we had a few years there in the beginning when we were first married but separated. .God promised me through the marriage that he would take care of everything. . and He did. . I have no regrets. . God was faithful to me and gave to me far above what I could ever ask or think. . . I got to have 6 children and never lost any in death. My children have loved me and cherished me through all of this. . They have loved and cherished Jim and honored him. They will honor his memory as I will. .

I feel Jim's presence with me and always will. . I will meet him in heaven and there we will live together. . I plan to keep on writing about the family. . Still so many more stories to be told. . Do please pray for my children. John especially is taking it hard today. . Dan and David and Mary, the 4 youngest, have taken it hard. . Jimmy, our oldest son, and Christian Joy are closer to me. . So now that I am ok they feel ok too. . I just don't want this grief to settle on my children. . They have beautiful families and they must go on . . I want them to have a good shot at life as I have had. . I want them to know the deep happiness and contentment that I had with Jim. . I have fought to make a godly foundation for them with my own life. I have lived for them and tried to be an example to them. . Yet I am not an end in myself. . They must go on and be the next examples of godliness. . Oh, that Papa loved his kids. . As I said before, "Papa's babies could do no wrong!!" Danny said, "Mom . . Dad would just tell me . . Dan do what is right." And Danny said, "That's what I am tryin' to do."

Dan made up a song that he sang at the Memorial called, "Lord save my soul." Danny got a new tattoo, a big one of course. It says, "Lord save my soul." Danny has a fire in him. . He will be another Wildman. . That young man is gonna be something for the Lord. . Also at the Memorial Jason sang 2 wonderful songs. . One was called, "Love songs to Jesus." And the other one was, "There will be no Depression in heaven." It was sung by the Carter family during the Depression years of the 30's. June Carter Cash's family sang this. . (Johnny Cash's wife's family.) Jason is Christian's young man . . He is the most wonderful man . . All the kids love him. . I dare not snag him and pin point him about being a Christian. . He is one but I think Christian Joy doesn't know it. . He is another wild man for sure. . And oh those styles from NYC. . Jason wore a nice suit with white tennis shoes. . The kind ya slip on?

99

No Regrets (Part 2)

And ya know, I wrote about Fred the Baptist and how he tried to get we Hultquists to straighten up and be good? Well in the end he was smilin' and said he thought the Memorial was wonderful. . Bless his heart . . God love him. . But boy we had a strategy if he hadn't been calm. . We didn't have to use it . . But we had plans for that ol' boy. . Yet in the end he loved us all up and we loved him, and all was well. . Of course Dan's punk rocker friends came . .God love 'em. . All of my tragedies are accompanied by Punk Rockers. . Tattoos and face piercings. .

One thing that happened at the Memorial that was extra funny was this. . Miss Charlotte's granddaughter McKayla and my niece Ashly. . They were so cute. . They are 7 and 8. . Oh such sweet lil' girls. . They took turns falling across my lap and crying. . Ashly would say, "Can I have a turn now??" McKayla was eating Doritos and crying between bites. . McKayla asked her Grandma on the way home. . "Well can't Jim come back?"

And Miss Charlotte explained to her that when someone goes to heaven they don't want to come back. . "He don't even want to come back?" McKayla says in horror. . She cried all the way back home in the car. She told her grandparents . . "Don't show me any Stop signs as I keep thinking that Jim's life stopped." Ashly also cried all the way home in her parent's car. She said Jim was like a Father to her. . Those lil' girls were so dramatic and sweet. . I told Miss C. . ."Just cherish her as she is and at her age . . . what a sweet lil' girl." . . But Jay . . Char's husband and Mckayla's grandpa kept trying to untangle McKayla from me. . Then once he got her loose she would come back to me. . So he would try to motion to her with his eyes to let me loose. . "Now Connie has others to talk to, " he told her. . Jim had given McKayla the book Black Beauty and she loved it. . She loves horses and talks about this book so fondly . . Both of these lil' girls are so intelligent. . Our Baby Rose asked, "Where is Grandpa?" Her Mom and Dad tried to explain to her that Grandpa was with Baby Chloe Faye in heaven. . Baby is only 2 and half and she said, "No, Grandpa is at the hospital.". . But we have many pictures of Baby and Grandpa together.   She will always know Grandpa loved her. . well I should go back to bed and get some sleep. . All is well and good!!

100

I am OK (Part 1)

Dear Mothers. . Good Morning. . I went to bed early last night so I hope I can get a good writing in today. . I have longed to make vegetable soup . . I am frying hamburger now. Jason, Christian Joy's boyfriend from NYC, didn't eat beef so I hadn't fixed any hamburger when they were here. . Oh we had enough food without cooking anyway. . But now I need to cook a bit . . Thank the Lord!!! . . I love my home and I am so glad to be here. . I long to do some homemaking today. . Papa would've wanted me to just go on. . Bless his heart he paid the house off and I have that. . But I called the Social Security office and found out that I will get no S.S. or Medicare. . HelllOOO? What's new? I will get Jims S.S. when I am 60 years old and that will be just 70 percent of it. . I just turned 59, so I have another year to wait to get that. . That's ok . . the devil won't take me down. . Ya know I am ok? I really am ok. .

And the Lord is my source of supply. I am weak but He is strong. . He won't leave me or forsake me. .

I am burdened for my dear friends. . They are all so sweet to me. . My dear friend Ruth was here yesterday afternoon. . . I am very weak but I think that is to be expected. . But when Ruth got home she called me to see if I was ok. . Jill seems worried too. . I am kind of delicate right now. . But my mind is on target and I am ok . . I have to rest a lot . . I just feel bad for my friends who seem so worried. . . But no one need worry. . You know the way I do things. . Mary L says I will probably fall into a million dollars. . I don't doubt that at all. . I think the biggest thing on my mind is the Revolution. . I know that sounds crazy. But ya know what? I tried to explain that to my friend Barb yesterday. . See I am not on any nerve pills or anything. . I take aspirin or whatever to calm down a bit. . But I sleep ok. . See I will show you who I am. . I am like a person who worked 10 hours a day and got that figured out. . And Jim dying is like someone telling me that I will have to work 15 hours a day. . And I say to them, "That's ok I am used to working." Well, see it's a spiritual work and I know how to work spiritually. . I know how to do this. . It's not strange to me to fall into diverse temptations. . Been there and done that. . . My burdens got heavier and I now have a bigger piece of land to plow. . But I get it. . I know how to do this. . Yes it's harder but it is not strange to me. . I do have more on my plate than I know what to do with but I know how to distribute it. . And I know I will have days where I feel lost and despondent?

But I have done that before. . I am not afraid. . I did need
nerve pills when Jim was in the hospital. But now I know he is
safe and sound . . I know he is ok and with Jesus. . I have no
children to look after. . They are all safely grown and happy. . I
have so much to be thankful for. . My Jesus has my address. .
And ya know I am ornery and plan on kickin' this world in the
back end before I die. . .

I guess if I am worried about anything I am worried that I
won't get to start a Revolution. Oh my goodness Chrissy and
Jason encouraged me a lot. . Ya know NYC is quite a place. . I
wouldn't want to live there but I like some of the free thinking?

One thing Jason said to me is that my Zine, or like an
e-newsletter, has to have something that will draw people. .

101

The Zine (Part 2)

Ya know, Jason and Chrissy and I had many valuable conversations. . Ones that I know the angels listened to. . Jason said that a lot of political ideas that weren't even right got off the ground because they had appeal. . And I said, "Ya know I want my Zine to have such a flavor of the underground. . . I want to put a writing out there that will give the housewife MOXIE and class. . I want them to feel good and ornery after reading my writings. . I want my Zine to go out to the streets of NYC. . Its gotta be mainly handwritten. . But ya know it just has to call the housewife. . I gotta do it!!! I just gotta do it. . Oh I have so much to do. .

Anyway after I get a good group of zines then I want to make a book out of them. . I want a book that is handwritten. . I mean mostly handwritten. . Have maybe a forth of it typed. . But I want it to have the flavor of the underground press. . I want it to be a secret wisdom. . Like reading words from a Secret Garden. . I can feel it coming. . Man does the devil hate it!!! But ya know I am getting' pretty old. . I won't be here that much longer . . Now my luck I will prolly live to be a hundred. . God forbid!!! . .

I love Papa and miss him . . I feel his presence here. . I am so happy that he loved me. . Ya know I was visiting with the kids . . . And I said "Ya know Papa never blamed me for anything? I mean he could have said I wasn't a good wife to him. . Or he could have blamed the kids for things. . But he never did. . His wife and kids could do no wrong." He over did it on blaming himself and we all hated that. . The kids loved him and wanted to talk to him about his past. . But he wouldn't talk about it with them. . They wanted to tell him that it was ok and they loved him anyway. ."Oh Papa we miss you and love you as you were . . just as you were. . I am ok Papa. . . all is well". . . And ya know now that he is gone I can allow myself to think of things that Papa didn't even want me to think about. . See I loved Jim . . when he was good or when he was bad. . Sometimes he was so bad he made me laugh. . The Lord cut me out to be his wife. . I am a lil' different because I followed a man who was different. . Papa wouldn't allow me to express much at times. And Papa about broke his neck tryin' to hide a lot of his past. . But to us it was like goin' around with an extra leg and pretending it wasn't there. . It was always as plain as the nose on my face but we couldn't talk about it. . it was a story that was always waiting to be told. .

Now Papa won't care if I tell it as Jesus will soothe him. . Papa was a walking book and I became a writer. I think my writing was really developed as I wrote hundreds or thousands of letters to Papa in prison. . of course he would burn them all before he would get out. . He was always tap dancin' and burnin' his bridges behind him. . He was a card right to the end. . And even at the hospital with all the tubes in him I would say to him. . "Wild man we ain't given up right? " And he would shake his head yes. . Eyes closed and unable to speak. . he shook his head, "Yes my dear wife we ain't given up". . But ya know folks like us who live on the edge sometimes fall over the side accidently. . We always gambled with life and it seems this time we got caught . . But we had a good life together. . Papa and me. . And the Lord gave me double blessings for all that we suffered. .

And ya know there is a woman for every man. . Some men take a lot of extra lovin' to awaken their hearts to the Lord. . The Dr. Dobson husband isn't that only one that is valuable. . Some of you ladies have husbands that aren't saved. . Well that doesn't mean that you don't have a real marriage. . Your husband is your mission. . Over and over again I tell my kids that Dad and I weren't married for almost 40 years because we were perfect people. . Just 2 good forgivers, that's all!! Ya gotta commit your life to your own husband and win his heart. . You gotta win him with your life. . Brow beating him to church to walk the aisle is silly...

102

Planning my Day

Dear Mothers, Well I am up planning my day. . Yesterday I made a big batch of goolash as I thought Danny may stop by. He didn't, but Mary did . . And as she got ready to leave she looked in the frig and saw the goolash. . "Oh Mom can I have this?" . . . So I gave it to her. . This morning I am washing my rag rugs and getting the house in order to start caring for little Baby David on May 1st. He will be about a month old when I get him. . .I have a porta-crib in my bedroom downstairs here. . . So I have to clean it all up and wash up some baby blankets that I have. . I want to just babysit this baby as I can live on what I will make. . I want to give Baby my undivided attention. Later on I hope I can get some tutoring jobs in my home. . I should be able to get some. . Just for a few hours a day. . Amy won't bring the baby until 9:30 each week day morning. . So I will have time to write and still start a commotion on the email machine. .

This morning I have a smile on my face. . I keep sensing Papa this morning and he is laughing. . I guess he is happy that I am not giving up. ." I am doin' my best Papa and I will see you again soon in glory.". . Oh my heart grieves and yet I must walk by faith. . I know the Lord has a wonderful plan in all of this. . I am not just saying this by faith. . I sense His hand upon me and I am excited to know what He will do with me. . I am so raw right now . . I feel like my husband has been ripped from my physical body. . I had to go to the Dr. and get nerve pills. .I didn't want to but was unable to sleep and was having panic attacks. . I have to keep going and be an example to my children. . I had the funniest Dr. at Urgent Care. . Ya wanna know how much they charge for an appointment for folks who have no Insurance? 97 dollars for the visit. . I mean this is for a poor person who can't afford insurance and is sick . . 97 dollars? Well I said something to the Dr. about it and he said, "Oh we aren't going to charge you 97 dollars"!!!! So he charged me 58 bucks. . Thank God I had the money. . But he was very nice to me in the Drs. office. . He asked if Jim had worked and I said he worked part time delivering pizza as he was 65. . This Dr. was quite a riot and he said, "Had I not become a Dr. I had wanted to be a Pizza Delivery guy." In the office I didn't laugh but I sure did once I got out of there. . What a riot!!

Well ya know there is some truth in that. . Papa and me were rich!! I feel kinda sorry, I guess, for some folks who have always lived by money. . Their lives are governed by how much money they have in their pocket. . How many times did Papa and me fly by the seat of our pants? With nothing but faith and a smile on our faces. . B.S.-in until we got some faith. . some real faith . . Often we lived on moxie and love and B.S.-in. . I wonder now as I am without Papa, can I carry on my B.S.- in' and make Papa keep smilin' at me outta heaven? . . . I hear his voice in my heart. ."Yes Connie you can do it. Just don't give up. . Take it a day at a time and quit confessing negative." Papa used to tell me, if I confessed something negative. . ."Now look at you, sayin' all that and you tell me not to." . . The kids always tease me if I say anything negative. ."Don't confess it." . Well like I said that is how we ran our home. . We could never afford to look at the obvious.

103

Never Give Up

Ya know today I got out Jim's wedding ring and put it on my cross necklace to wear around my neck . . Oh wow this ring is worn thin and tarnished. .When we first got married I had gotten him a nice wedding ring. . But a few years into the marriage, Wild Man threw the ring away in the ditch one day as he hitchhiked out of town. He was to leave me many times before he gave his heart to the Lord. . . Each time he came back home by faith, I would forgive him and buy him another wedding ring. . Somehow he threw them all away. . After many hard years of marriage, he had gone through many wedding rings. . I was ready to give up. . Jill encouraged me to go buy yet another wedding ring for Jim. . I said it was gonna be a super cheap one as I wasn't sure he wouldn't throw that one away also . . I had so little faith left and I was so losing my heart of courage. . But I used the little faith I had and bought a really cheap wedding ring at K-Mart. . Jim later was healed, saved, and delivered by the mighty hand of Jesus. . About 10 years later I told him I wanted to buy him a nicer wedding ring but he wouldn't have it. He wanted the ring I had bought as it was special to him. . the one he kept. . He never took it off unless he had to. . Then at the hospital before he died they gave the ring to me. . I will always wear it around my neck. . Oh it is so old and tarnished . . just such a cheap ring. . So special to me as it was the ring Papa kept. . The one I bought with so little faith and the ring he wore for the last 26 years. .

God had promised me double blessings for all I had suffered and Papa wore this ring through these blessed years. . This wedding ring of Papa's is so dear to me as it hangs over the cross on my necklace. . The cross is really pretty and bright and the ring is so old and worn thin. . But each time I look in the mirror to comb my hair, I see my necklace and I think of Jim and my faith and how faith is so loved by God. . Even though we feel worn out and feel we can't go another step . . we must go on by faith. . Even though our hearts may be heavy, we must do the next thing by faith. . Even though nothing but hard things are in our past, we must expect good things up ahead. . it is impossible to please God without faith. . .. And all things are possible with God.

The Letters

{Part III}

- April 2013 Reflections -

104

A Simple Evening Supper (Part 1)

Dear Mothers, Jim loved a simple quiet supper. . We would be busy all day and maybe upset about something. . But by the end of the day, Jim would turn the News on TV and I knew it was time to be quiet. . So I would go out to the kitchen and start Supper.

One meal Jim loved in the evening was Baked Beans with wieners. . .I would get out my big cast iron skillet and put a lil' oil in it . . .Then throw in the whole package of wieners and fry them. . You could use the turkey wieners if you like them better. . After these are fried, then I would get out a bowl and put in 3 cans of pork 'n beans. . drained. . To this I would add about a forth cup of ketchup and a half cup of brown sugar and a good squirt of mustard. . sprinkle some salt on it and some black pepper. . . .Stir this up good. Then put all of this into the skillet with the hot dogs. . Stir this up. . then put this in the oven to bake about 20 minutes, or until it bubbles. . On the top of this I would put a slice of green pepper and onion before I put in the oven. . Jim wouldn't eat an onion or green pepper, but he liked them like this. .

Honestly Jim would eat this meal for supper and as a snack later in the evening . . usually we had just bread and butter with it. . Just a Simple Supper. . .

105

A Quiet Evening Supper (Part 2)

I forgot to say too about the baked beans and wieners. . I would often fix Jim a baked potato to go with this. . This was after the children had married and moved away and it was just Jim and I. . And I have written many times about the Hamburger Gravy I made for the Wild man. . I loved to be quiet in the evening, in my kitchen, and make Papa's coffee and stir the Hamburger gravy. . Once you make the Gravy you gotta stand there and stir it or it would burn. But it was peaceful in my kitchen as the sun went down on another day with my Darling Jim. . .

Often I just felt locked in to our own world. . We had lived a life that no one could hardly understand . . A life we tried to explain . . But at the end of the day, we didn't have to explain anything more for that day. . Often we turned off the phone. . and watched some show on tv. . I would get out my sewing and quietly mend something . . I loved to hand sew. . it seems there is a rhythm of life in hand sewing that you miss out on when you use a sewing machine. . .

106

Jim's Winter Gloves (Part 3)

I should be writing about Spring but it's still so cold . . . it is warming up. . But as I was writing the last part about mending in the evening. . I was thinking of Papa's winter gloves. Jim had to walk to work so he needed warm clothes. . Well we had paid quite a bit for these gloves so they had to last the winter. . Well each night he came home from work, the gloves would be torn in the palms . . . we couldn't afford new gloves. . So each evening I would sew his gloves together again and have them ready for the next morning.   By the time Spring came, and he didn't need the gloves. . I got to looking at them one day after he had gone to work. . There was nothing but stitches holding his gloves together. . It looked impossible that they could even keep his hands warm.   Only stitches held us together. . Like prayer stitches. . Lil' miracles of thread. . .

This was way before Jim came to the Lord.   This was when he walked to work and we didn't have a car. . We only had one child at the time. . But as the warm weather came and I looked at the gloves laying on the table as they had played their part for the winter. . . I thought as I looked at all the stitches in the gloves that it did mean something. . . It was sort of a picture of our lives. . . The tears and the mending each day. . We were put together with Love and that was about all. . . But Jesus saw us and kept us going. . Two accidents going someplace. . Papa at his worst trying to tell me he loved me by walking to work in the cold. . And me trying to tell him I understood by mending his gloves every winter evening.

And yet we were both so fragile from the trials of life, we had only love to live on. . and each day we tried to do what was right and what said, "I love you".. ..He was to leave me many times after this. . . And his deliverance came about 9 years later. . But somehow God continued to give us faith in Him .. By the everyday miracles, He kept us together in Him. .

. . . Love, Connie

Appendix

107

The Above Rubies Marriage Testimony

[This article first appeared in Above Rubies Magazine, #53, in September 2000, under anonymous. It was republished in the February 2013 edition, #86, along with an update.]

"Bring him Home!"

Jim and I met in 1966. He was 25, I was 18. He was wild and so was I. When we met he had already been in and out of prison for about seven years, and was going back again for two years. We married in the prison six months later. Soon after I had our son. A few months later I miraculously came to Christ. Because of the prison term I didn't live with my husband for another two and a half years. After being home a year he began a crime spree.

He deserted us over and over again. I had nowhere to turn except to God. No one knew where my mate was. Some of the time my heart would rage like a forest fire out of control on the dry and windy land. I would run and scream like a woman out of her mind searching for her mate in the raging fire. I'd scream curses at God only to faint from exhaustion and weep bitter tears of repentance. I'd get back up, begin running again and fall again and again until finally I'd surrender my will to Christ's will. And then I'd wait, maybe for another six months, knowing God was in control.

In the beginning I thought about divorce. Well, wasn't that what a woman does if her husband leaves her repeatedly? And yet Jim kept coming back and repenting. He would mysteriously end up at my back door after being missing for four or five months, looking like a mad man. But beneath the dirt and sun-parched face he was still mine.

I'd bring him in the house, give him dinner, and speak peace and rest to him. I'd run the bath water for him to wash and feel like a man again. Compassion would rise up in my heart. I had the Lord, and my Jim didn't. I would reverence and praise him.

I would shut the door on the world and be alone with my mate. No matter what he had done to me, we were still one flesh. He was my first and only husband--a terrible, ungodly, unfaithful husband, but he was still my husband. His healing came again and again as I forgave him and opened my love to him. I held nothing back.

There would be times when putting dinner on the table, I'd notice he was awfully late. I'd listen for the car and begin running again and again to the window. The old familiar fear would rage, knowing that he had deserted me again. This scene happened about 30 times in the first twelve years of marriage. He would suddenly disappear without warning. The children would run in from play crying, "Where is daddy, where is my daddy?" I'd tell my little baby, Jimmy, "Daddy is sick, but Jesus is going to heal him." I taught my little ones to pray, "Thank you, Jesus, for bringing my daddy home."

His mother died and no one could find him. My prayers went out to God day and night, seemingly to no avail. The years went on and the crimes continued as if I had no God. I felt like a motherless and fatherless child. I was completely exhausted and my mate committed still another crime and went to prison for almost four years.

I loved him. I felt he was demon possessed and yet he was my husband. At times I hated him. Your arms and legs belong to you even when they hurt, you can't cut them off. I was like this about my husband. He was mine. I hated it when he deserted me, but I was married to him no matter what. Adultery to me was the worst of all sins. At night before I entered my marriage bed alone I'd cry out to God to keep me pure, even in my dreams, and that I would never dream of another man.

Many mornings I'd wake up and think, "Lord, why did you give me another day to live?" Often the world seemed so black to me, but sweet Jesus would come to me and speak life and joy into my tired and depressed soul. One time God supernaturally took all my burdens away. I forgot he had left me. It was so hilarious. I even wrote myself a note to remember to pray for him.

The day-to-day message from the Lord was, "Now Connie, you just get up out of that bed. You straighten your shoulders and you believe God. This problem isn't bigger than God. Don't you prepare your day as though Jim won't be home. You get up and prepare your home for a miracle." Each evening when my husband was gone I'd fix supper for him and put his plate at the head of the table. No one was allowed to sit in his chair and no one was allowed to bad mouth him. I ran the house as if he were home.

I survived and lived on the Word of God. I whispered His name all day long. He walked with me in the valley of death and guided me to a straight path.

All our phone conversations at the prison were censored. I'd speak faith into the phone and say, "I'll see you in a few days, honey. The guards thought we were planning an escape because Jim had been given a 10-year sentence!

People laughed at me and said that he would always leave me and be in and out of prison. The prison guards told me that

Jim was institutionalized and was hopeless. Hopeless or not, he was my husband. I knew I could never forsake the Lord by not forgiving my own husband. Also, as a young wife I wanted to be a teacher of women when I got older and I knew I couldn't be divorced. I'd sing, "Keep me Jesus as the apple of thine eye."

The Lord would tell me to speak to the mountains in my life and not doubt in my heart. I would speak to the mountain, which was Jim. I would woo him and call him home with my prayers. Every muscle in my body cried out to God to save him. I fasted and prayed continuously.

Jim was healed in 1979. After he had been in prison for the last four years and home for about three months, he asked me to have another baby, our fourth. I was so fearful and yet was praying for Jim to be healed. I said No. I was not going to have another baby. I walked away from him and the Lord spoke to me. "Connie, He said, "You have come this far by faith. Don't give up now." After much heartache I obeyed the Lord my God.

"Yes," I told Jim, I'll have another baby for you." I placed my future in his hands. When Jim saw that I still believed in his life as a human being something released within him. The fear left his eyes and He was delivered. He lifted his hands up to His Father and received the anointing of a sound and unfettered mind. He began to slowly give more and more of his life to Christ. He took over the bills and began to work steadily.

The Lord did exceedingly and abundantly more than I could ask or think. He gave me joy unspeakable. He showed me He was there all the time. Satan had come in like a flood but the Lord raised such a standard against him. All Satan did was build me a grand testimony.

God gave me a new batch of fruit. I had David in 1980, Dan in 1982 and Mary in 1985. We now have six children. I was queen in my palace. I raised the children for Christ and to honor their daddy. I taught them to jump when daddy walked into the room. I taught them to get Daddy a cup of coffee or honor him in some way.

The guys at work say to my husband, "You don't go out and drink and party." Jim says, "I have a wife to go home to. I spend my time with my family."

One guy said, "Boy, when work is over you run home." The guy thought something was wrong with him!

I sit here thinking of Jim and the man he is now. He has been home sitting at the head of our table for 20 years! Who is this Jesus we serve? Surely He is the Son of the living God, a God who saw me crying and feeling so forsaken, a God who knew the very moment Jim would be healed. Jim is my walking miracle to always remind me that nothing is impossible with God. He showed me that if we don't give up we will see the glory of God.

Proverbs 31:11 says, "The heart of her husband doth safely trust in her." A woman must gain the trust of a man such as this. His healing comes as he feels safe enough to give Christ his heart and his wife his heart. When Jim was healed he went from not seeing me to taking care of me. He turned from Satan and took dominion over his Eve. He came into his responsibilities as a man. I come under my husband and I don't desire to do anything else. I don't always agree with him and I tell him I don't. But in the end his word is final. I want to be as Esther and not as Queen Vashti.

Dear wives and mothers, don't give up give up on your husband. He sees your heartache. He won't leave you or forsake you if you trust in Him. I know for I've been to the other side.

UPDATE TO BRING HIM HOME--Updated December 2012

In April 2006 my dear husband, Jim, died of a heart attack. As my six children and I gathered around Jim's hospital bed the Hospital Chaplain told me, "I have never seen a family so full of love." As the nurse told us Jim had passed, I whispered to each of the children to comfort and love each other. As we left the hospital room I left a chapter in my life.

I wish I could say that all went well after that, but grief is hard to understand, and unpredictable. Jim and I were married for almost 40 years, my first and only husband. I still live in our family home, garden, bake bread, cook from scratch, and try to practice what I preach.

Jim would often say, "Connie and the children are what I live for, but I try to put God first. My family is my life." When we would give our testimony to a church group Jim would look up from the pulpit and say, "If it wasn't for that little girl right over there I wouldn't be alive today. She was my guardian angel."

I now have nine grandchildren and they are a wonderful blessing. Had I given up on my husband I would have never felt the joy of having all of these grandchildren. Praise the Lord.

Jim and I lived from one miracle to the next. To me, Jim and I were just two good forgivers as we all have feet of clay. Our love and life together was the most gut wrenching experience I ever had, but it was a one of a kind marriage. Would I do it all again? Yes, I would. Oh yes, it was worth it all. My marriage was tried in the fires many times but I came out with a testimony of love and truth. My marriage has a message, "If you don't give up you will see the glory of God."

- *Mrs. Connie Hultquist*

Connie and Jim on their wedding day (at the Prison) in 1966.

Visit Connie on the world wide web at:

Website: "Happy Housewifery"

http://happyhousewifery.com

Blog: "A Revival for Homemakers"

http://conniehultquist.blogspot.com

For more titles from The Legacy of Home Press,
please visit our site:

http://thelegacyofhomepress.blogspot.com

Made in the USA
Middletown, DE
19 November 2021

52949087R00186